Starting Out Right

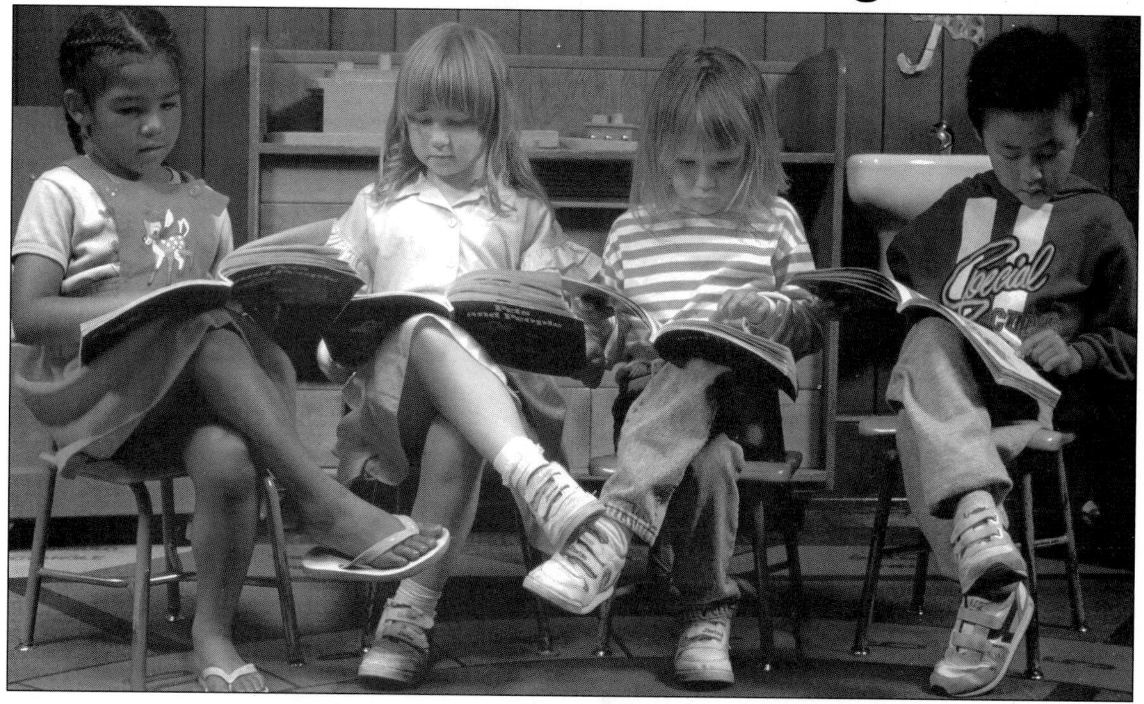

A Guide to Promoting Children's Reading Success

NATIONAL ACADEMY PRESS • 2101 Constitution Avenue, NW • Washington, DC 20418

NOTICE: The project that is the subject of this report was approved by the Governing Board of the National Research Council, whose members are drawn from the councils of the National Academy of Sciences, the National Academy of Engineering, and the Institute of Medicine. The members of the committee responsible for the report were chosen for their special competences and with regard for appropriate balance.

The study was supported by Contract/Grant No. H023S50001 between the National Academy of Sciences and the U.S. Department of Education. Any opinions, findings, conclusions, or recommendations expressed in this publication are those of the author(s) and do not necessarily reflect the views of the organizations or agencies that provided support for this project.

Committee on the Prevention of Reading Difficulties in Young Children

CATHERINE SNOW (*Chair*), Graduate School of Education, Harvard University; MARILYN JAGER ADAMS, Bolt, Beranek, and Newman, Inc., Cambridge, Massachusetts; BARBARA T. BOWMAN, Erikson Institute, Chicago, Illinois; BARBARA FOORMAN, Department of Pediatrics, University of Texas, and Houston Medical School; DOROTHY FOWLER, Fairfax County Public Schools, Annandale, Virginia; CLAUDE N. GOLDENBERG, Department of Teacher Education, California State University, Long Beach; EDWARD J. KAME'ENUI*, College of Education, University of Oregon, Eugene; WILLIAM LABOV, Department of Linguistics and Psychology, University of Pennsylvania; RICHARD K. OLSON, Department of Psychology, University of Colorado, Boulder; ANNEMARIE SULLIVAN PALINCSAR, School of Education, University of Michigan, Ann Arbor; CHARLES A. PERFETTI, Department of Psychology, University of Pittsburgh; HOLLIS S. SCARBOROUGH, Brooklyn College, City University of New York, and Haskins Laboratories, New Haven, Connecticut; SALLY SHAYWITZ, Department of Pediatrics, Yale University; KEITH STANOVICH, Ontario Institute for Studies in Education, University of Toronto; DOROTHY STRICKLAND, Graduate School of Education, Rutgers University; SAM STRINGFIELD, Center for the Social Organization of Schools, Johns Hopkins University; ELIZABETH SULZBY, School of Education, University of Michigan, Ann Arbor;

M. SUSAN BURNS, *Study Director*; PEG GRIFFIN, *Research Associate*; SHARON VANDIVERE, *Project Assistant*

* Did not sign off on this book

Library of Congress Cataloging-in-Publication Data

Starting out right : a guide to promoting children's reading success / M. Susan Burns, Peg Griffin, and Catherine E. Snow, editors ; Committee on the Prevention of Reading Difficulties in Young Children, Commission on Behavioral and Social Sciences and Education, National Research Council.

p. cm.

Includes bibliographical references and index.

ISBN 0-309-06410-4 (pbk.)

1. Reading (Early childhood)--United States. 2. Reading disability--United States. I. Burns, M. Susan (Marie Susan). II. Griffin, Peg. III. Snow, Catherine E. IV. Committee on the Prevention of Reading Difficulties in Young Children.

LB1139.5.R43 S83 1998

372.1--ddc21

98-25492

Additional copies of this report are available from National Academy Press, 2101 Constitution Avenue, NW, Lockbox 285, Washington, DC 20055.

Call (800) 624-6242 or (202) 334-3313 (in the Washington metropolitan area).

This report is also available online at **http://www.nap.edu**

Printed in the United States of America

Book design by Francesca Moghari (National Academy Press).

First Printing, January 1999
Second Printing, May 1999
Third Printing, September 1999

Starting Out Right

A Guide to Promoting Children's Reading Success

M. Susan Burns, Peg Griffin,
and Catherine E. Snow, *Editors*

Committee on the Prevention of Reading Difficulties in Young Children

Commission on Behavioral and Social Sciences and Education

NATIONAL RESEARCH COUNCIL

NATIONAL ACADEMY PRESS
Washington, DC 1999

Contents

Foreword

Madeline soon ate and drank.
On her bed there was a crank,
and a crack on the ceiling had the habit
*of sometimes looking like a rabbit.**

How easy it is for us adults to forget the magic of our own childhood—the freshness of each discovery, the joy at awakening to each new day. And yet the human spirit thrives on the stimulation that comes from discovering new things, and each of us is refreshed by an active imagination that truly exercises the mind. We began this brief foreword with a quotation from a well-known children's book to help transport the reader, for just one fleeting moment, into the mind of a young child. As he or she reads or is being read to, the series of vivid images that accompanies a good story will carry a child into unfamiliar worlds—leading the child to make new mental connections that will enrich the experience of many subsequent actual events.

Yet today we are seeing an increasing number of students who are not proficient readers, as well as adults who cannot read well, even though they have been to school. In fact, surveys tell us that 4 in 10 children experience literacy problems. It is for this reason that the National Research Council of the National Academies of Sciences and Engineering, with which we are both involved, set out to identify the specific skills and experiences that children need to become fluent readers. A select committee composed of educators, linguists, pediatricians, and psychologists has carefully reviewed the relevant scientific literature about how children

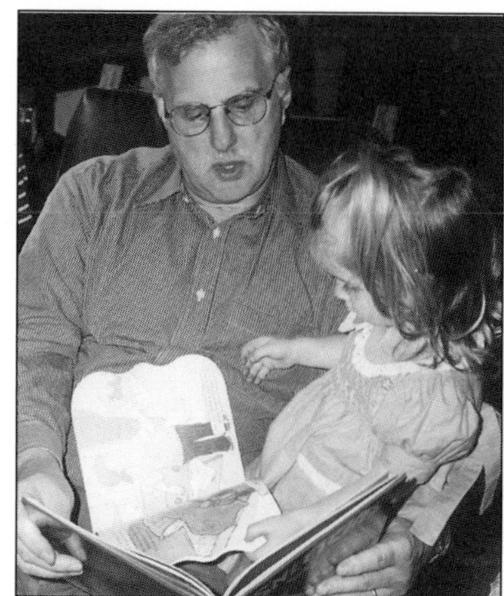

become successful readers, and their findings are reflected in this book, which is based on the groundbreaking study *Preventing Reading Difficulties in Young Children.*

In our society, reading is essential for creating a healthy mind and for building the capacity needed for a lifetime of learning. It is therefore our hope that this book—and others like it—will be prescribed by pediatricians, as part of their responsibility to help parents raise a healthy child. Many parents who read this book may be surprised to learn of research suggesting that infants only a few months old should be read to, as part of the preparation they will need much later for reading—or that reciting nursery rhymes is an important part of reading preparation. As parents and grandparents, we have found that reading out loud with our younger family members creates a strong bond between generations, providing us with many shared experiences to enjoy. We remember reading to our children even after they had become excellent readers, allowing us to explore literature together. In retrospect, we now realize that the obvious enjoyment of these sessions helped our children to view reading as a very pleasurable experience.

Our friend Dr. Vartan Gregorian, former president of the New York City Public Library, has said:

> "Any book creates for the reader a place elsewhere. A person reading is a person suspended between the immediate and the timeless. This suspension serves a purpose that has little to do with escaping from the real world, the sin avid readers are most commonly accused of. Reading provides renewal. What is renewed is the imagination."

No person should be deprived of one of life's real pleasures, the joy of reading.

Bruce and Betty Alberts

Bruce and Betty Alberts have four children, including a foster child who joined the family at age 13. They have 3 grandchildren ages 2 to 7, plus one more on the way. They look forward with great eagerness to visits with grandchildren, which provide them with an excuse to enjoy reading children's books once again. In addition to his family responsibilities, Bruce Alberts is president of the National Academy of Sciences.

---

*From Bemelmans, L. (1939) *Madeline.* New York: The Viking Press.

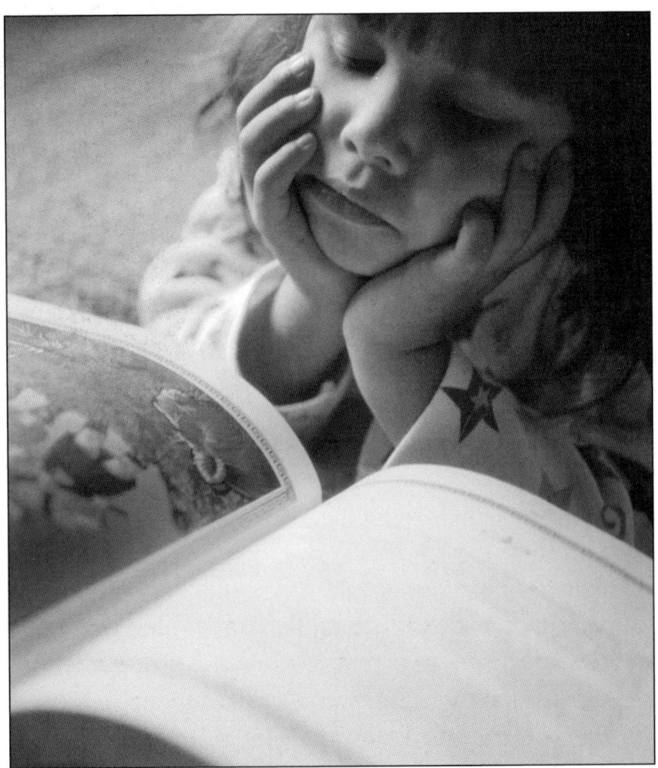

This book is based on a major report of the National Research Council, entitled *Preventing Reading Difficulties in Young Children*, prepared by the Committee on the Prevention of Reading Difficulties in Young Children. Both books are available on the Internet at **www.nap.edu**.

Introduction

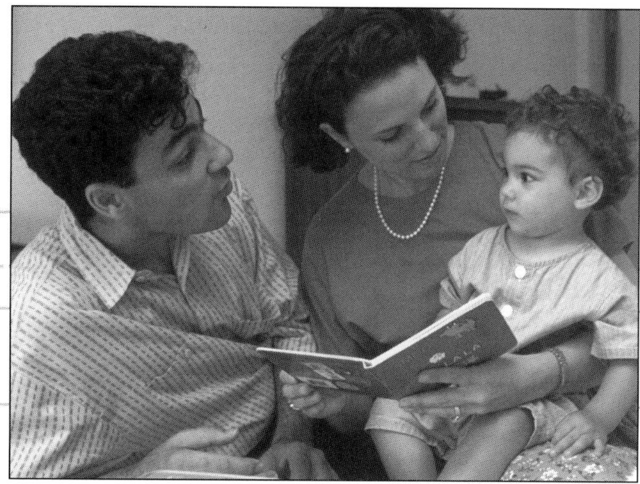

Parents want to provide their preschool children with a good start in literacy. A school district tells its teachers to change the way they teach reading. Preschool caregivers want to be sure that the children they care for are ready for school. A mother attending a school meeting hears confusing messages about the best way to teach beginning reading. A corporate executive wants the company to support an after-school tutoring program, but is not sure where to start.

This book is for all these people. It is written particularly for parents, who should find the information useful in making judgments about:

- **what kinds of language and literacy experiences to look for in preschool and child care settings,**
- **what to look for in initial reading instruction in kindergarten and the early grades,**
- **what to ask school boards, principals, elected officials, and other policy makers who make decisions regarding early reading instruction,**
- **whether their child is making progress in reading related skills and early reading.**

It is also for others who can influence the education and development of young children, especially policy makers, caregivers, and teachers.

Editors' Note: Two icons appear frequently throughout this book

Activities that can be done with children   i "For More Information" see page 153

The goal of *Starting Out Right* is to share, with a broad audience, a wealth of knowledge based on a summary of extensive research. i The book focuses on children from birth through the first years of formal schooling, and our hope is that the findings it contains will be widely used to improve their reading and educational prospects. To this end, these pages include practical guidelines, program descriptions, advice on resources, and strategies that can be used in everyday life, including:

- **practical literacy and language activities for parents and their young children and**
- **activities and practices for classrooms.**

We caution that most of the activities could be used to excess. Consider as an example the statement that "the more you read with your children, the more they will learn to love reading." In this book we emphasize that reading to young children is important for language and literacy growth—but it can be overdone. After several days of too many hours of reading every day, the reading experience might well start to become distasteful for a child.

The language and literacy activities included in this book illustrate the underlying concepts important for reading that are supported by scientific research. Many of the activities are familiar, and they are here to connect what readers may already know to unfamiliar-sounding concepts such as "phonological awareness." Our hope is that, through these activities, the nature of each literacy concept—along with ways to support its development and to look out for problems—will become clear. We expect that the individual activities included will be helpful for most children; however, they are examples rather than comprehensive curricula in themselves. For many activities, we provide a list of resources for obtaining comprehensive curricula on teaching a concept. The glossary on page 147 gives basic definitions of unfamiliar reading terms found throughout the text.

GUIDE TO THIS BOOK

This books consists of five chapters. We know that some readers may only have interest in one particular chapter. For example, the parent of a child about to enter first grade may be most interested in the chapter on *Becoming Real*

Readers. Although this chapter can certainly be read immediately after this introduction, it is also true that reading the chapter on *Growing Up to Read* will help in clarifying how your child got to this point. Likewise, we suggest that parents of preschool children should also read about the early grades, to gain perspective on where they are headed. And we suggest that people with an interest in preventing reading difficulties—family and community members, school administrators, district leaders, teachers, curriculum decision makers, volunteer tutors, and elected officials—read the entire book. Please note that we sometimes refer to a parent, when in fact a teacher or early childhood professional may be the adult participating in the activity. And, we sometimes use the word teacher when in practice it might be a parent participating in the activity.

INTRODUCTION
The content and purposes of the book

PROMOTING CHILDREN'S READING SUCCESS
Brief introduction to the process of reading

GROWING UP TO READ
What children need in order to arrive at school prepared to learn to read

BECOMING REAL READERS
Elements of effective classroom instruction in kindergarten and the early grades

PREVENTING READING DIFFICULTIES
Addressing reading difficulties: Issues of urgent concern for parents, teachers, school administrators, district leaders, curriculum decision makers, policy makers, and elected officials

GLOSSARY — FOR MORE INFORMATION — INTERNET RESOURCES — INDEX

Promoting Children's Reading Success

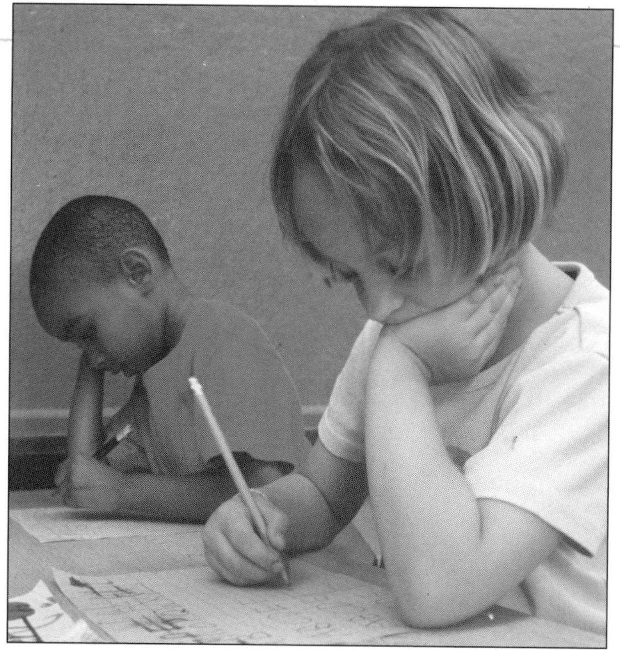

Why is a book like this needed? A devastatingly large number of people in America cannot read as well as they need to for success in life. Large numbers of school-age children, including children from all social classes, face significant difficulties in learning to read. An increasing proportion of children in American schools, particularly in certain school systems, are considered learning disabled; most of the children are so identified because of reading difficulties. Failure to learn to read adequately for continued school success is especially likely among poor children, among children who are members of racial minority groups, and among those whose native language is not English. Achieving educational excellence for all requires an understanding of why these disparities exist as well as serious, informed efforts to redress them.

We are most concerned with the children in this country who do not read well enough to meet the demands of an increasingly competitive economy. To be employable in the modern world, today's high school graduates must be able to read challenging material and use printed matter to solve problems independently. In the United States, we should expect 100 percent literacy from our population.

In the past, ideologies and narrowly focused beliefs have made it difficult to implement genuine reforms in reading instruction. The teaching of reading evokes passions like few other subject areas. Often the debate has been heated,

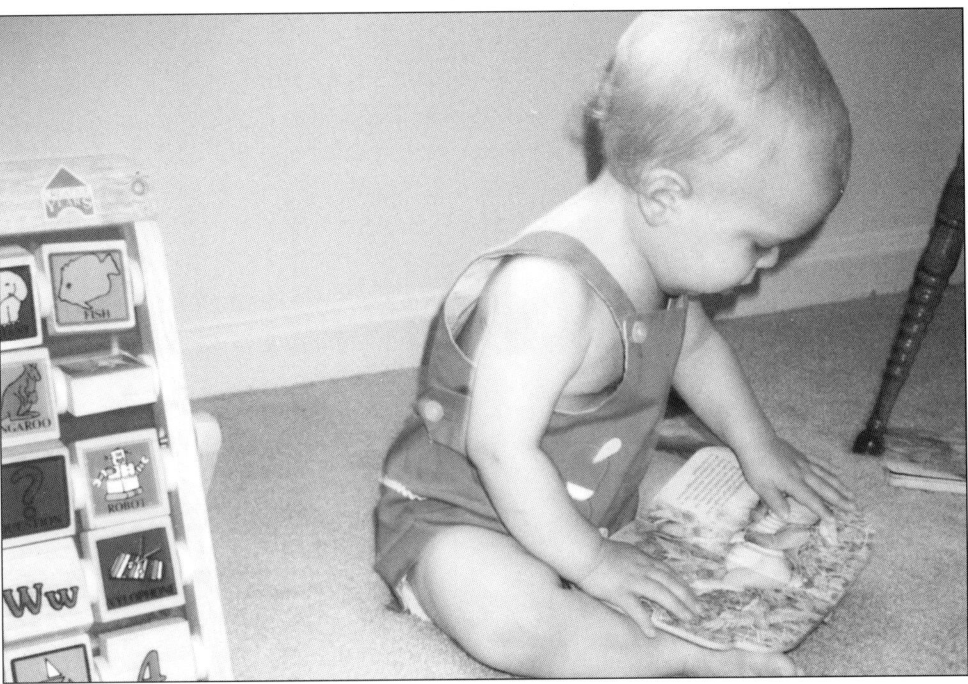

and parents and educators have been understandably frustrated by school districts and states that shift curricula to embrace the latest solution. In fact, there is no simple solution. This is one of the most important messages of this book.

Reading is a complex and multifaceted process, and children need an approach to learning that integrates many elements. Children who are first learning to read need appropriate help in understanding, learning, and using the spelling-sound conventions of the writing system, as well as opportunities to appreciate the information and pleasures offered by print. They need to learn more and more about the vocabulary and sentence structure of written English. They need help with procedures for monitoring comprehension. They also need sufficient practice with a variety of texts to achieve fluency, so that both word recognition and reading comprehension become increasingly fast, accurate, and well coordinated. Three main accomplishments characterize good readers:

- **they understand the alphabetic system of English to identify printed words,**
- **they have and use background knowledge and strategies to obtain meaning from print,**
- **they read fluently.**

In good instruction, these three goals are not only addressed but are also well integrated, enabling young readers to gain proficiency in all of them.

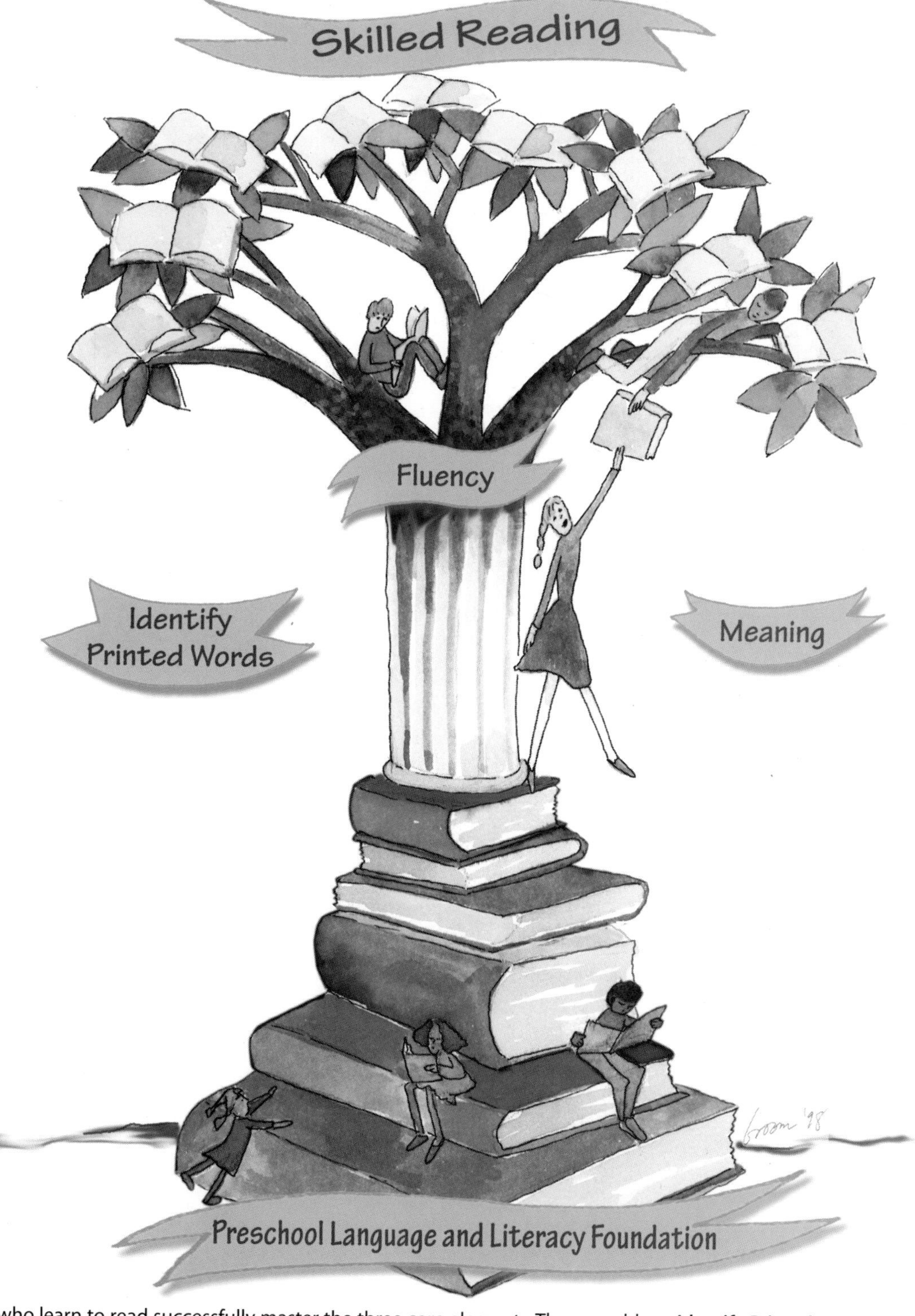

Children who learn to read successfully master the three core elements. They are able to **Identify Printed Words** using sound spelling connections and have a sight word repertoire. They are able to use previous knowledge, vocabulary, and comprehension strategies to read for **Meaning.** They read with **Fluency**, that is, they can identify words swiftly so that what is read is understood and reading itself is enjoyable. Children start to accumulate the skills needed for reading early in life—building a **Preschool Language and Literacy Foundation**—which includes opportunities for children to develop oral language skills, including phonological awareness, motivation to read, appreciation for literate forms, print awareness, and letter knowledge.

CIRCUMSTANCES THAT PROMOTE READING

During the first months and years of life, children's experiences with language and literacy can begin to form a basis for their later reading success. The ideal time to begin sharing books with children is during babyhood, even with children as young as six weeks. Research consistently demonstrates that the more children know about language and literacy before they arrive at school, the better equipped they are to succeed in reading. Main accomplishments include:

- **oral language skills and phonological awareness,**
- **motivation to learn and appreciation for literate forms,**
- **print awareness and letter knowledge.**

These language and literacy accomplishments are achieved best through activities that are integrated across different developmental areas, that is, cognitive development, fine and gross motor development, social and emotional development, and language development.

Given the opportunity, young children develop vocabulary, other language skills, and basic knowledge about the world around them. They know what books are and how they work. They are enthusiastic about reading and are beginning to explore being readers and writers. They have opportunities to learn about letters and the structure of words.

Vocabulary, language skills, and knowledge about the world are acquired during interesting conversations with responsive adults. Talking about books, about daily happenings, about what happened at day care or at work not only contributes to children's vocabularies, but also increases their ability to

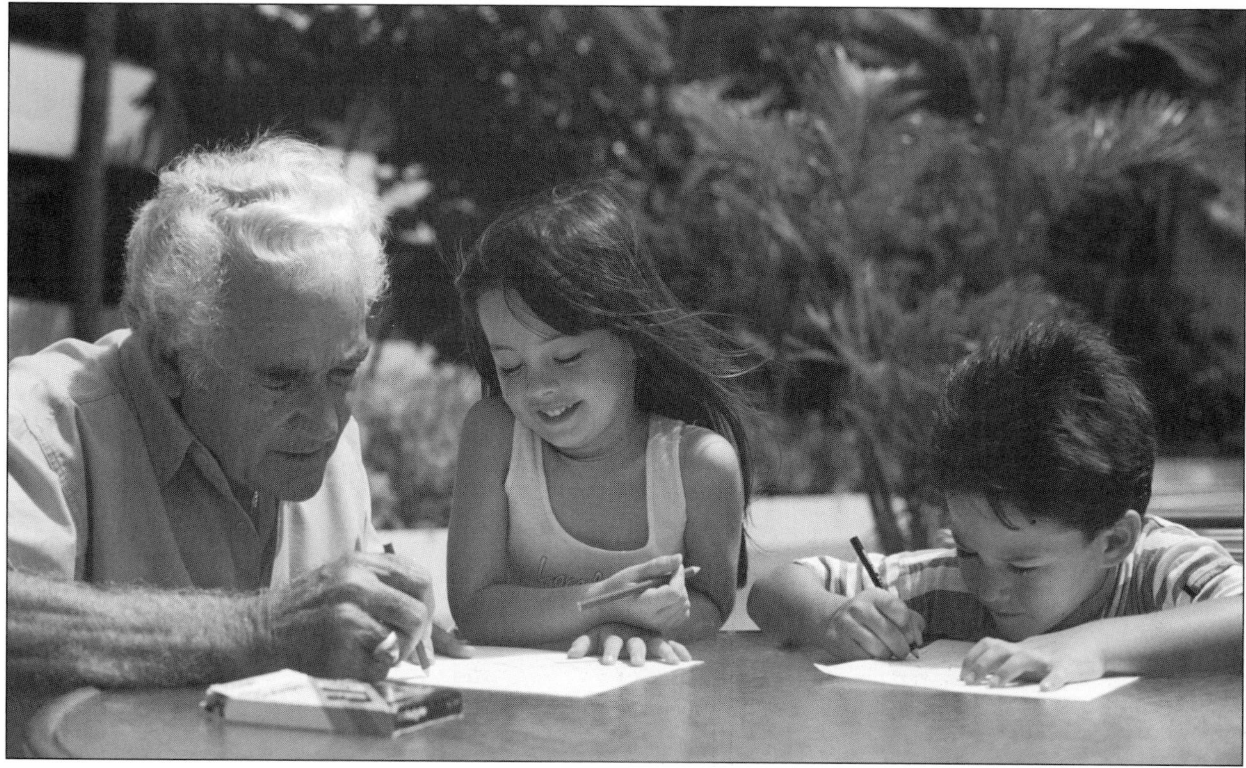

understand stories and explanations and their understanding of how things work—all skills that will be important in early reading.

Knowledge about and love for literacy can develop only through experience. Children should own books, should have access to books in their preschool and primary classrooms, should be read to often, and should see others reading and writing. Understanding the value of literacy as a means of communication, as well as coming to love book-reading as a time for emotional closeness, are accomplishments typical of the future good reader.

The committee's larger report emphasized the importance of phonological awareness—not to be confused with phonics. When children achieve phonological awareness, they are able to think about how words sound, apart from what words mean. For example, they appreciate that the word "kitchen" has two spoken parts (syllables), that the word "bed" rhymes with "bread," and that the words "cat" and "king" begin with the same sound. Children can and should develop some degree of phonological awareness in the preschool years, because it is a crucial early step toward understanding the alphabetic principle and, ultimately, toward learning to read.

Another necessary circumstance for reading success is, of course, excellent reading instruction once children begin school. Although there is no single reading program out there to solve all problems, we do know that the most

Reading Instruction in Kindergarten Through Third Grade

Recommendations on the mechanics of reading:

- Kindergarten instruction should be designed to provide practice with the sound structure of words, the recognition and production of letters, knowledge about print concepts, and familiarity with the basic purposes and mechanisms of reading and writing.
- First grade instruction should be designed to provide explicit instruction and practice with sound structures that lead to phonemic awareness, familiarity with spelling-sound correspondences and common spelling conventions and their use in identifying printed words, "sight" recognition of frequent words, and independent reading, including reading aloud. A wide variety of well-written and engaging texts that are below the children's frustration level should be provided.
- Instruction for children who have started to read independently, typically second graders and above, should be designed to encourage children to sound out and confirm the identities of visually unfamiliar words they encounter in the course of reading meaningful text, recognizing words primarily through attention to their letter-sound relationships. Although context and pictures can be used as a tool to monitor word recognition, children should not be taught to use them to substitute for information provided by the letters in the word.
- Because the ability to obtain meaning from print depends so strongly on the development of accuracy in word recognition and reading fluency, both of the latter should be regularly assessed in the classroom, permitting timely and effective instructional response when difficulty or delay is apparent.

Recommendations on comprehension:

- Kindergarten instruction should be designed to stimulate verbal interaction, to instruct vocabulary, and to encourage talk about books.
- Beginning in the earliest grades, instruction should promote comprehension by actively building linguistic and conceptual knowledge in a rich variety of domains.
- Throughout the early grades, reading curricula should include explicit instruction on strategies such as summarizing the main idea, predicting events and outcomes in upcoming text, drawing inferences, and monitoring for coherence and misunderstandings. This instruction can take place while adults read to students or when students read themselves.
- Conceptual knowledge and comprehension strategies should be regularly assessed in the classroom, permitting timely and effective instructional response when difficulty or delay is apparent.

Recommendations on writing:

- Once children learn to write letters, they should be encouraged to write them, use them to begin writing words or parts of words, and to use words to begin writing sentences. Instruction should be designed with the understanding that the use of invented spelling is not in conflict with teaching correct spelling. Beginning writing with invented spelling can be helpful for developing understanding of phoneme identity, phoneme segmentation, and sound-spelling relationships. Conventionally correct spelling should be developed through focused instruction and practice. Primary grade children should be expected to spell previously studied words and spelling patterns correctly in their final writing products. Writing should take place on a daily basis to encourage children to become more comfortable and familiar with it.

Recommendations on reading practices and motivation:

- Throughout the early grades, time, materials, and resources should be provided (a) to support daily independent reading of texts selected to be of particular interest for the individual student, and also beneath the individual student's frustration level, in order to consolidate the student's capacity for independent reading and (b) to support daily assisted or supported reading and rereading of texts that are slightly more difficult in wording or in linguistic, rhetorical, or conceptual structure in order to promote advances in the student's capacities.
- Throughout the early grades, schools should promote independent reading outside of school by such means as daily at-home reading assignments and expectations, summer reading lists, encouraging parental involvement, and by working with community groups, including public librarians, who share this same goal.

Adapted from *Preventing Reading Difficulties in Young Children* (National Academy Press, 1998)

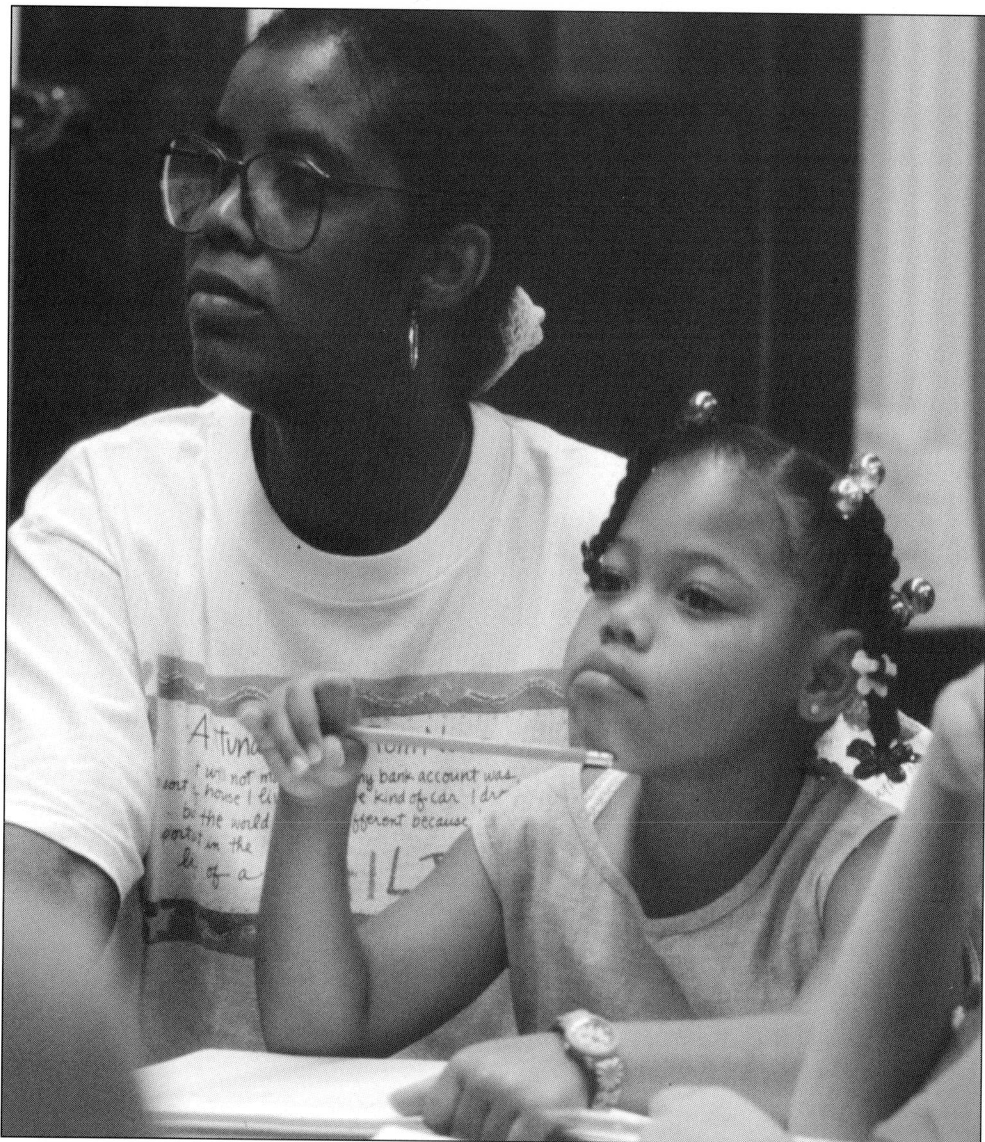

effective programs share certain common features. Formal instruction in reading needs to focus on the development of two sorts of mastery: word recognition and comprehension. In *Preventing Reading Difficulties in Young Children* (National Academy Press, 1998), we make recommendations for reading instruction for kindergarten through third grade. The concepts included in these recommendations, along with those relevant to preschoolers, toddlers, and babies, are those that we will clarify and illustrate throughout this book.

The majority of reading problems faced by today's adolescents and adults could have been avoided or resolved in children's early years. That is one reason why this book is partly addressed to policy makers, such as school superintendents, district leaders, and elected officials. If we, as a society, are to prevent

reading difficulties among the current generation of children in America, we must provide them with opportunities to:

- **explore the many uses and functions of written language and develop mastery of them,**
- **understand, learn, and use the relationships between the spellings of words and the sounds of speech to recognize and spell written words,**
- **practice and enhance vocabulary, language, and comprehension skills,**
- **have adults read to them and discuss and react to the literature,**
- **experience enthusiasm, joy, and success in learning to read and write,**
- **use reading and writing as tools for learning,**
- **receive effective prevention programs as early as possible if they are at risk of potential reading difficulties, and**
- **receive effective intervention and remediation programs, well-integrated with their everyday classroom activities, as soon as they begin to have difficulty.**

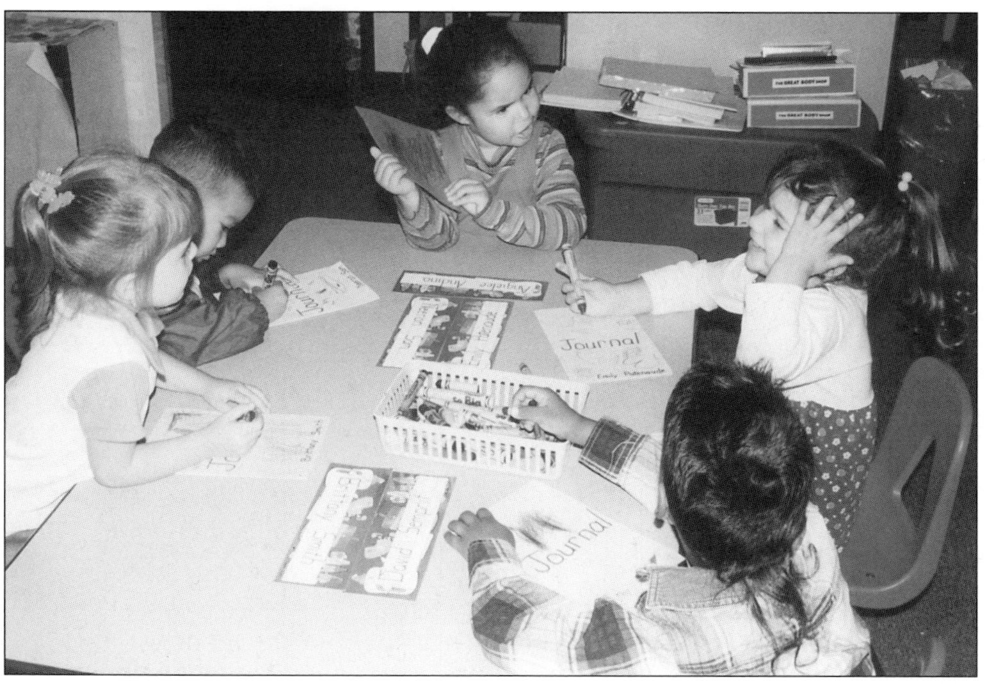

For the most high-risk children, enriched preschool environments and excellent primary grade instruction can be a deciding factor between success or failure that will follow them all their lives. That is why this book focuses mainly on early childhood environments and primary grade instruction. No time is as important, or as fleeting, as a child's early years of life and schooling. Herein lies our greatest hope, and our most practical and effective opportunity for prevention.

Throughout the book we have tried to include the voices of a wide range of people—teachers, parents, pediatricians, volunteer tutors, and researchers. We also have provided vignettes of effective programs and interventions from around the country.

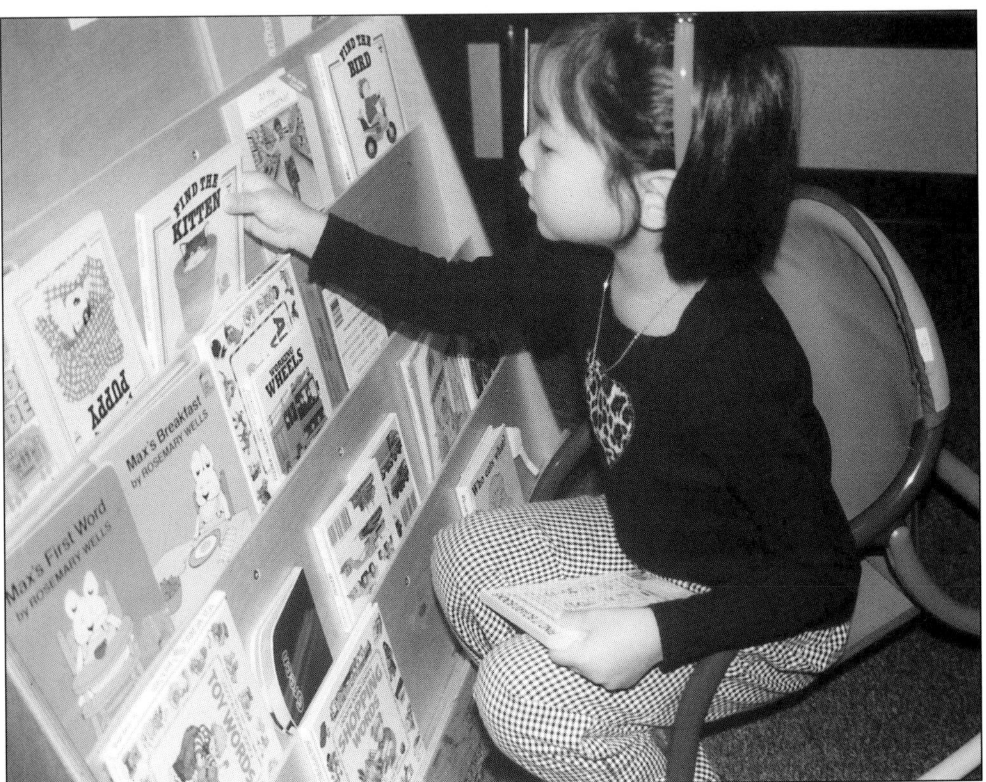

Growing Up to Read

Birth Through Age Four

Children begin to develop their language skills in infancy. Even their babbles and coos and the ways their families speak to them before they really understand can help them to become speakers of their native tongue. When an infant shows excitement over pictures in a storybook, when a two-year-old scribbles with a crayon, when a four-year-old points out letters in a street sign—all of these actions signal a child's growing literacy development.

The more children already know about the nature and purposes of reading *before* kindergarten, the more teachers have to build on in their reading instruction. Research reveals that the children most at risk for reading difficulties in the primary grades are those who began school with less verbal skill, less phonological awareness, less letter knowledge, and less familiarity with the basic purposes and mechanisms of reading.

To prepare children for reading instruction in the early grades, it is best that they be exposed to high-quality language and literacy environments—in their homes, day care centers, and preschools. The best time to start sharing books with children is during babyhood, even when they are as young as six weeks. In this chapter, we offer concrete examples, activities, and ideas for how families, early childhood educators, health care professionals, and communities can bring literacy into the lives of young children.

Everyday Literacy: One Family Home

Promoting literacy at home does not mean creating an academic setting and formally teaching children. Parents and other caregivers can take advantage of opportunities that arise in daily life to help their children develop language and literacy. Often, these are unplanned, casual acts, like commenting on words on an article of clothing or engaging children in conversation. At other times, it is a conscious effort to read good books with children or provide toys that promote good literacy development.

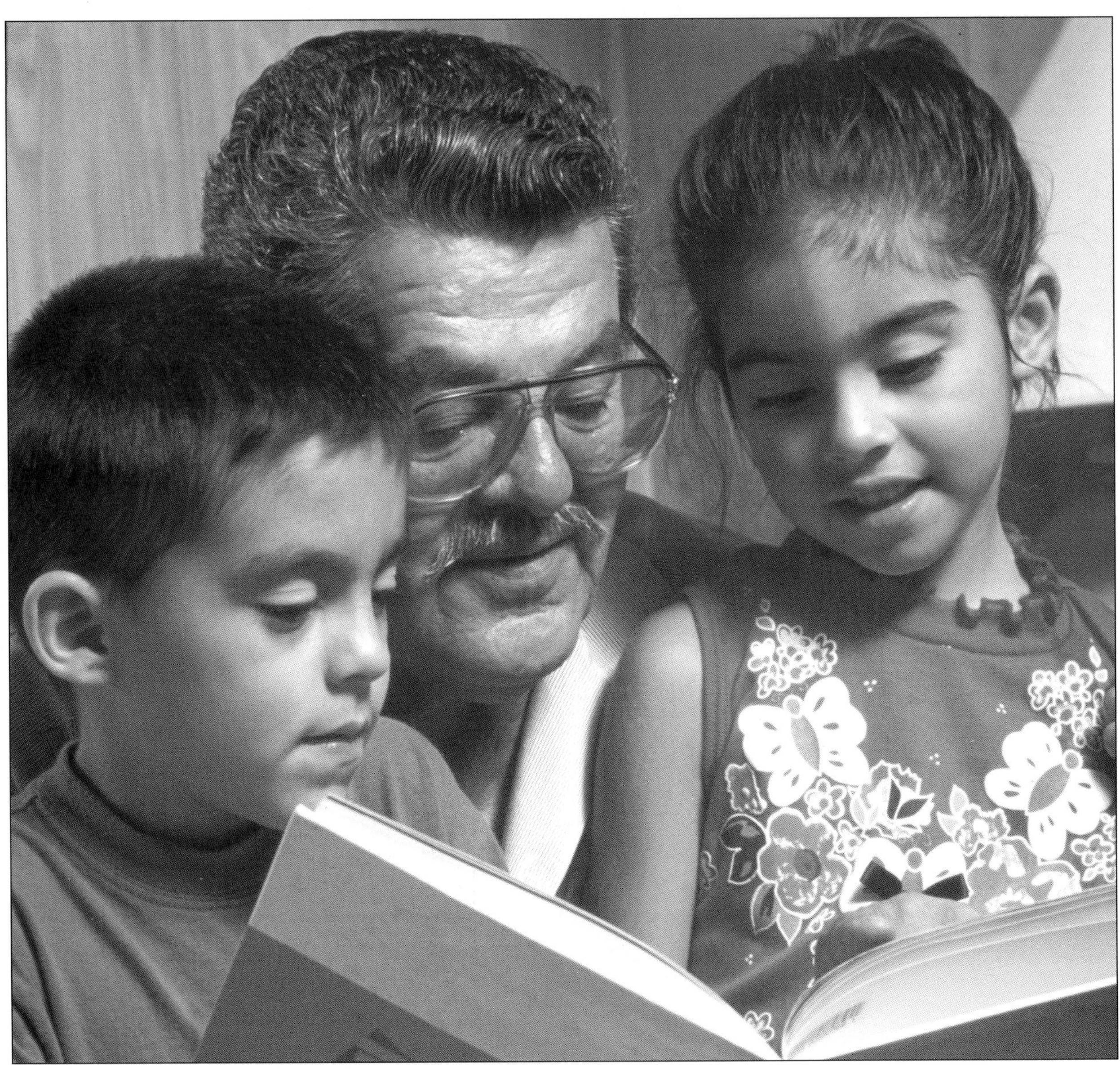

Three-year-old Carlos has just awakened from a nap and is lying on the floor, not fully awake yet. His older sister Rosa has been watching TV and is playing with her blocks and dinosaurs in the living room. Although their home is modest, these children have what they need to promote good language and literacy skills: a simple but appropriate array of toys and books and, most importantly, attentive parents.

In the corner there is a little bookshelf with 20 or so children's books, including 3 that are due back to the library the next day. (The children go to the library with their mother at least once a month.) There are puzzles, a magnetic board with letters, and, in a canvas bag, some plastic farm animals—treasured for pretend play. Dad is sitting on the sofa, reading the newspaper. In a few hours, the children's mother will come home from work, and he will leave for his job as a night-shift security guard.

Dad takes the children into the kitchen for some juice and crackers. Although he has several chores to finish, he makes the effort to ask if they want to hear a story.

"Yes!" The children respond in enthusiastic unison.

"Let's read *Tacky the Penguin,"* cries Carlos.

"No, I want the caterpillar," Rosa whines.

Before they can continue arguing, Dad steps in. "Cut it out, you guys. We'll read them both. We read *The Very Hungry Caterpillar* last time, right? So this time, let's start with Tacky."

The children seem satisfied with this. After their snack, they march into the living room and sit on either side of their father, who begins to read the story of a funny penguin named Tacky. They listen intently, sometimes asking questions about pictures or words that catch their attention. The father is responsive, answering when he can, or simply saying that he doesn't know.

Having heard songs from birth, young Rosa has come to love the rhythm of language. She is so engrossed that she recites the ends of rhyming lines and claps the beat as her father reads. After they finish Tacky, they turn to *The Very Hungry Caterpillar*.

"Okay, guys. I've got some stuff to do. You can play here or in your room. No fighting, okay?" Dad goes to the kitchen table with a stack of bills and begins to write checks.

Little Carlos is fast on his heels. "I want to do it!"

"You want to write?"

"Yeah."

Dad gives him a blank piece of paper and a not-too-sharp pencil. "Okay, sit here and write with me."

Carlos climbs on a chair and begins to make squiggles on the paper.

"Hey, buddy, that's pretty good," Dad says encouragingly. "What else can you write?"

Carlos sweeps his finger slowly across his squiggly lines. "Carlos," he pronounces, slowly and deliberately. He is imitating his older sister, who knows how to write her name.

He writes a little longer, then joins his sister in the living room, who by this time has tired of blocks and dinosaurs and is holding a favorite book. Rosa knows many by heart and recites them, as if she is actually reading. Carlos listens attentively.

Suddenly aware of her audience, Rosa holds the book up, as her prekindergarten teacher does, and "reads" to her younger brother, suddenly switching to a louder recitation voice. After a few minutes, Carlos proclaims, "I want to read!"

"Carlos, you can't read yet," replies Rosa, a little impatiently. Suddenly, there is the sound of a key in the latch.

"Mom's home!" cries Rosa. She drops the book, and both children run to the front door. As Mom arrives, Dad says goodbye and hurriedly leaves for work.

Early research dating back to the 1930s suggested that there was little use in teaching children how to read until they had already conquered specific readiness skills, such as certain fine motor skills and the ability to tell right from left. Today, researchers know more. They know that growing up to be a reader depends mostly on the child's knowledge about language and print. A wide range of experiences with printed and spoken language, from infancy through early childhood, strongly influences a child's future success in reading. What is good for a six-year-old, however, is not necessarily good for a three-year-old. Children need activities they will enjoy and can succeed at, without being pushed uncomfortably beyond their current developmental stage. Even when children cannot yet spell, they learn from trying to write. Even when children cannot yet read, they learn from being read to.

The following pages describe key aspects of language and literacy for children from birth through age four, along with activities that can be woven into daily life. In this section, we address parents, teachers, uncles, aunts, grandparents, babysitters, and day care providers—in short, everyone who is important in the child's life, everyone who cares, everyone who is willing.

Key Aspects of Language and Literacy, Activities for Very Young Children

Extended Vocabulary and Language Development

Children who are exposed to sophisticated vocabulary in the course of interesting conversations learn the words they will later need to recognize and understand when reading. Vocalization in the crib gives way to play with rhyming language and nonsense words. Toddlers find that the words they use in conversation and the objects they represent are depicted in books—that the picture is a symbol for the real object and that the writing represents spoken language. In addition to listening to stories, children label the objects in books, comment on the characters, and request that an adult read to them. In their third and fourth years, children use new vocabulary and grammatical constructions in their own speech. Talking to adults is children's best source of exposure to new vocabulary and ideas.

Activities

Labeling games are just right for little ones, for example, "Where is your nose?" Verbally label objects and events in your child's world, for example, "Nina is on the swing." Encourage your child to label objects and events, helping him or her with vocabulary and pronunciation. Do these types of labeling games with pictures in magazines, books, etc.

During necessary routines like baths, reading, and eating, be sure to make time to talk with children. Turn off the car radio and talk while you drive together. Watch children's TV programs together and talk about them. Instead of channel surfing, turn off the TV and use the time to talk.

As adults, we sometimes view conversation as a luxury—an extra in our busy lives. But for young children whose developing minds are striving to become literate, talk is essential—the more meaningful and substantive, the better. Set aside a regular "talk time" for adults and children, when having conversations about their lives is your main focus.

When you take your child on outings, surround these new experiences and events with lots of comments, questions, and answers between you and your child. Talk about what you are going to do before you do it and, afterward, talk about what you did. Structure these conversations to encourage the children to do more of the talking by asking questions and sharing interest in your child's thoughts and opinions. Support your child's efforts to communicate complex thoughts by waiting patiently, suggesting words as needed. Let your child sometimes control the subject of the conversations, and encourage her or his efforts to use new words and to describe complex or distant topics.

Pick books that connect to a child's life and talk about those connections. For example, when you read *Green Eggs and Ham* you might ask your child, "What color eggs do you eat?" "Shall we look for purple eggs in the store?"

Try turning the tables during reading time. When most adults share a book with young children, they do the reading and the child does the listening. But once children reach preschool age, parents and teachers can encourage them to become the reader or teller of the story instead. Start by prompting the child to say something about the book. (You can get the ball rolling by asking a question or making a comment yourself.) After the child responds, rephrase his or her answer and expand it by adding information. Continue along in this manner, each time, encouraging the child to expand further on the narration.

blink
black
blood
blow
blob

Phonological Awareness

During the preschool years, most children gradually become sensitive to the sounds, as well as the meanings, of spoken words. They demonstrate this phonological awareness in many ways; for instance: they notice rhymes and enjoy poems and rhyming songs; they make up silly names for things by substituting one sound for another (e.g., bubblegum, bubblebum, gugglebum, bumbleyum); they break long words into syllables or clap along with each syllable in a phrase; they notice that the pronunciations of several words (like "dog" and "dark" and "dusty") all begin the same way.

Although younger preschoolers rarely pay attention to the smallest meaningful segments (phonemes) of words, gaining an awareness of these phonemes is a more advanced aspect of phonological awareness that becomes increasingly important as school approaches, because these segments are what letters usually stand for. That's the alphabetic principle. A child who has attained phonemic awareness, for example, understands that there are three phonemes in the spoken word "mud." Many activities can nurture phonological awareness in the preschool years.

Activities

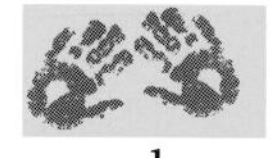

Songs, rhyming games, language play, and nursery rhymes—these are all excellent ways to spark children's awareness of language and sounds.

For example, sing the Teddy Bear song. 

Teddy bear, Teddy bear, turn around.
Teddy bear, Teddy bear, touch the ground.
Teddy bear, Teddy bear, show your shoe.
Teddy bear, Teddy bear, that will do.

Teddy bear, Teddy bear, brush your hair.
Teddy bear, Teddy bear, climb the stair.
Teddy bear, Teddy bear, reach for the sky.
Teddy bear, Teddy bear, wave goodbye.

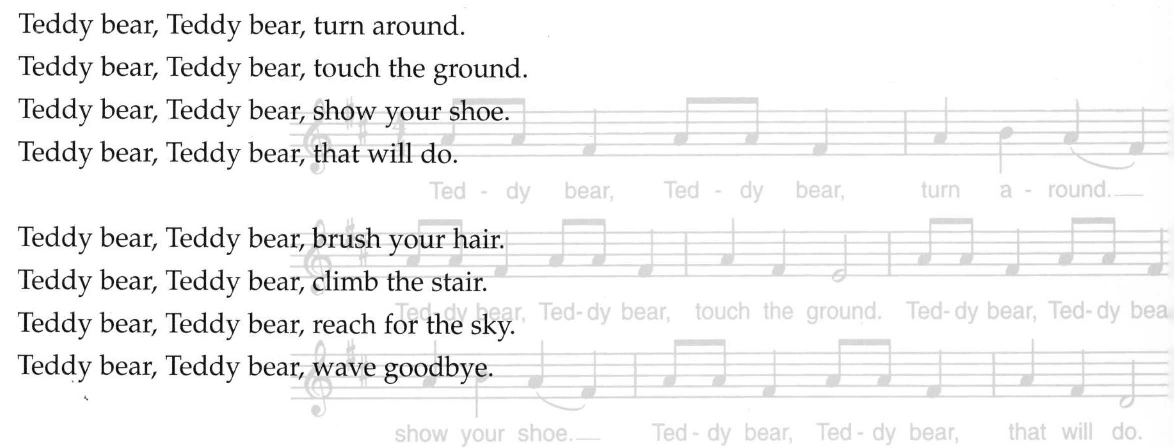

Take advantage of everyday activities to talk about words and sounds. For example, when buying fruit at the market, you might ask the child which sound is the same in the words *peach* and *pineapple*, or in *peach* and *tea.*

Choose some books that focus on sounds. For example, the Dr. Seuss books can lead to lots of chanting and fun with sounds—but don't let the author do all the work. Invite the child to supply the last word of each rhyme. Follow the model the book provides and make some silly rhymes that are special for each child.

Make up your own games with rhyming words, silly sounds, and chants, like this one:

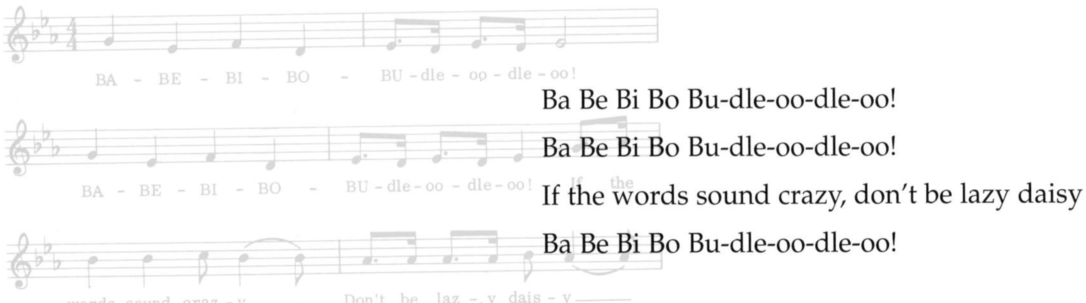

Ba Be Bi Bo Bu-dle-oo-dle-oo!
Ba Be Bi Bo Bu-dle-oo-dle-oo!
If the words sound crazy, don't be lazy daisy
Ba Be Bi Bo Bu-dle-oo-dle-oo!

Have fun creating new verses by substituting different consonants for the letter B. If the child's name is Sam, use "his" letter: Sa Se Si So Su-dle-oo-dle-oo!

Or try this traditional song made famous by the children's performer, Raffi.

Apples and Bananas

I like to eat eat eat apples and bananas.
I like to eat eat eat apples and bananas.

I like to ate ate ate aypuls and baynaynays.
I like to ate ate ate aypuls and baynaynays.

I like to eet eet eet eeples and beeneenees
I like to eet eet eet eeples and beeneenees

I like to ote ote ote opples and bononos.
I like to ote ote ote opples and bononos.

I like to ute ute ute upples and bununus.
I like to ute ute ute upples and bununus.

Falling in Love with Words

"Comfortable." How I loved that word, the meaning, the times to use it, the rolling jumble of consonant sounds. If only I could pronounce it! Though I tried and tried again, only strange sounds came from my mouth, "comdafable" or "cofdumfable." Sometimes I got so mad I threw a tantrum. Why could everyone say it but me?

My mother, amazingly in tune with my spirit, gave me a great approach. "Remember," she said. "Comfortable has two parts: comfort and table." She had me practice the parts, then say them fast together. So comfort-table it was—a bit funny with the long "a" in table, but oddly enough, that didn't bother me—it was a wonderful reminder of my mother helping me. After a while, I just started saying the word the same way everyone else does. But to this day, I always say "comfort" and "table" under my breath when I am writing or typing the word.

Years later, I still marvel at how easily my mother seemed to help me get ready to become a reader. By teaching me things like how to say "comfortable," she helped me understand that a word is not just something that lets you say what you mean, but is also a thing with a form and substance. A word is something you can take apart and put together. This is a key insight in word attack for reading. It's not just the meaning you attack, but the form.

Of course, as it turned out, "comfortable" has more than two parts when it comes to reading the letters. But my mother's advice was a great start on the central idea that you can think of and talk about a word separate from what it means. She helped me fall in love with words.

Speech Discrimination

Most young children can accurately perceive the difference between similar-sounding words ("coat" and "goat," "three" and "free," "witch" and "wish"), even though they may mispronounce words quite often in their own speech. Clearly, if a child cannot reliably make such distinctions, it will be difficult for him or her to engage in activities that help to develop phonological awareness, described above.

Activities

A simple game of pointing to pictures can be used to confirm that speech discrimination is reasonably accurate in a 3- to 5-year-old child. In a quiet place, show the child the array of pictures on page 25.

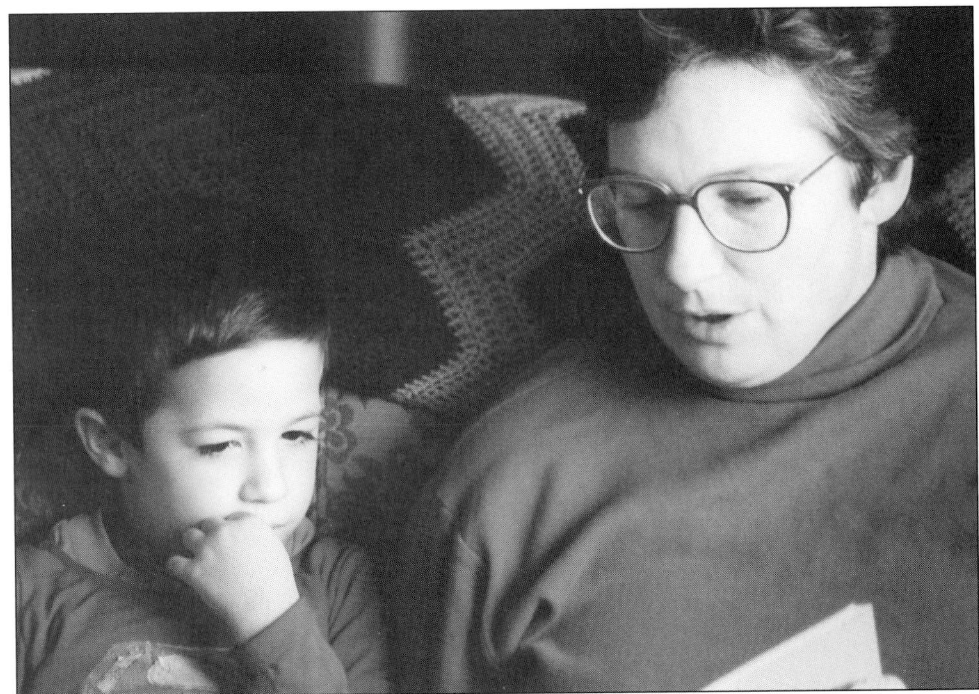

Speaking very clearly, say "Listen carefully. Show me the ________," filling in the blank with a word from the list below. (For fun, you can sometimes let the child quiz you by naming a picture for you to find.) The words are printed here in similar-sounding pairs, but you should jump around, not asking for the two members of a pair in succession. Ask only for words that you're sure are in the child's vocabulary, and don't do this when the child has a bad cold or ear infection.

If the child makes more than a few errors, repeat the exercise several weeks later. If performance is not any better, this could indicate a difficulty in hearing or speech perception, and a more thorough evaluation of these skills could be conducted by a professional speech pathologist. States provide early identification, screening, and assessment services as part of the Individuals with Disabilities Education Act. Contact your local school system for more information regarding these servics.

Show me the:

socks—fox	mouth—mouse	tea—key	cone—comb
pear—bear	clown—crown	fan—van	tie—pie
watch—wash	tower—towel	girls—curls	ring—wing

Knowledge of Narrative

Once children reach school age, stories will become a central part of their reading classes, so it is helpful for young children to become comfortable with narrative and its elements, such as characters, dialogue, and "what happens next." Young children are sensitive to sequence in language, such as following directions, and to sequences of events in stories.

Activities

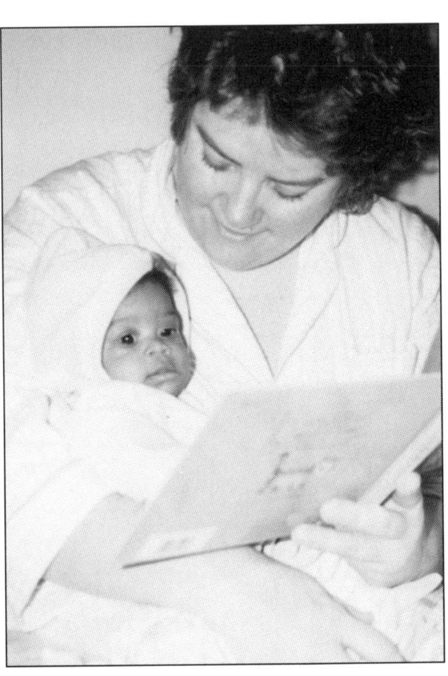

Storybooks: From infancy on, mothers, fathers, babysitters, uncles, aunts, grandparents and day care workers can help children learn about narrative simply by reading and enjoying good storybooks with them. Storybooks can be shared anywhere—at the breakfast table, in line at the supermarket, on the bus, and, of course, at bedtime. Daily reading periods can be brief but frequent for very young children. Encourage children to start to pretend to read by listening attentively, making appreciative comments, etc. Encourage children to start these emergent reading events by saying, "Now how about you read to me?" or "Your turn," after a book has been read (and liked) numerous times.

Oral storytelling: Children also learn about narrative through the oral stories they hear in the world around them. When they witness one adult telling another, "You'll never believe what happened to me on the way to the store," they begin to learn the magic, fun, and purpose of stories. Tell children some of your own stories, about when you were a child, or about your own parents or grandparents. With encouragement, parents and teachers can get children to tell of their own adventures in the form of a story. Encourage children to tell about special events, like holidays or trips. Use photo albums to remember and prompt these kind of stories.

Pretend storytelling: Puppet shows and formal storytelling events are thrilling and valuable experiences for children. But at home

Everyday Narrative and Dinner Conversations

Children learn about narrative when they hear their own personal experiences fed back in the form of stories, told in past tense, with themselves or people they know as main characters. They learn that certain happenings are noteworthy and make better stories then others—such as surprises, exciting events, or unexpected twists in daily life. At this family dinner table, a three-year-old boy hears his mother telling a story about his day. By the end of the meal, he has taken over the job.

It's dinner time. Three-year-old Matthew has his head down over a bowl of pasta, which he is vigorously slurping. His mother and grandmother sit beside him discussing the events of their day—work problems, errands done, good news about people they know.

"But how about Matthew?" asks the grandmother. "How was Matthew's day?"

"Well," starts his mother, "Aunt Lisa took Matthew out early this morning to go to storytime at the bookstore. But when they got there, they found out that the storytime was canceled."

"Oh no," replies Grandma sympathetically.

"So Aunt Lisa made a special day of it, and took Matthew down to the river for a ride on the ferry boat."

Matthew—who up until now appeared to be paying no attention—suddenly looks up from his bowl, cheeks covered in marinara sauce. "Matthew ride on a boat!" he exclaims. "Water goes splash!" he cries, waving his arms up in the air.

"I'll bet you saw some big buildings in the city," says Grandma.

"Big buildings. Up to the sky," answers Matthew, tilting his head back as though he still can see them.

"Then," continues the mother, "Aunt Lisa and Matthew ate lunch in the city. And then they got back on the boat and came home."

"And give ticket to the man," adds Matthew.

The mother and grandmother both remark on what a fun day it must have been and Matthew adds a few more details—some real, and some made up (like the cup of coffee he now claims to have drunk.) Later, in his bath, he and his grandmother act out the major parts of his "story," using toy boats in the water and two rubber ducks—one for Aunt Lisa, the other for Matthew—riding in the boat on their little adventure.

---

and at school, children also benefit from acting out stories that have been read to them using their own simple puppets or dolls. The action often goes well beyond the original story line. Also, encourage children to talk about books they already know and ask them to elaborate or add to the story line with their own creations, such as new endings or new circumstances for characters.

Book and Print Awareness

A child's sensitivity to print is a major first step toward reading. Young children can begin to understand that print is everywhere in the world around them, and that reading and writing are ways for them to get ideas, information, and knowledge. Children quickly settle into book-sharing routines with primary caregivers. Infants often kick their feet, make eye contact, smile in response to your talking,

Key Aspects of Language and Literacy, **Birth to Age Four**

and look where you point, as you read the book and share the pictures. Toddlers start recognizing favorite books by their cover, pretend to read books, and understand that books are handled in certain ways. As they reach their fourth year, children increasingly come to understand that it is the print that is read in stories, and that this print contains alphabet letters that are a special category of visual items, different even from numbers. They recognize print in their home, their neighborhood, and other local environments. i

First Attempts: Pretending to Read—Emergent Reading

"Goodnight Moon, by Margaret Wise Brown," proclaims a three-year-old girl, who pretends to read the cover page and author's name. With great relish, she opens the book and recites much of the book from memory.

Her mother knows that she is not yet reading the print but encourages her just the same. Intuitively, she suspects what has been found by research to be true: that children who pretend to read at this early age are more likely to become successful readers later.

"...and a picture of the cow jumping over the moon," continues the girl. She lifts the book close to her eyes and scrutinizes the print on the page. "A-B-A-B-Z," she recites, while pointing to the word "cow." This is an important connection. Already, she knows that words are made of letters that can be named. She resumes the story word for word, turning pages slowly. "Goodnight noises everywhere," she whispers, then suddenly shifts her voice, loudly pronouncing "The End" and proudly snapping the book shut.

Key Aspects of Language and Literacy, Birth to Age Four

Activities

At home, at day care, at preschool, provide print-rich environments, including access to high-quality books i, writing materials, and toys like alphabet blocks and alphabet refrigerator magnets. High-quality books are different for young children of different ages. For example, it is best to use cloth or cardboard books for babies because they will chew on the ones they like.

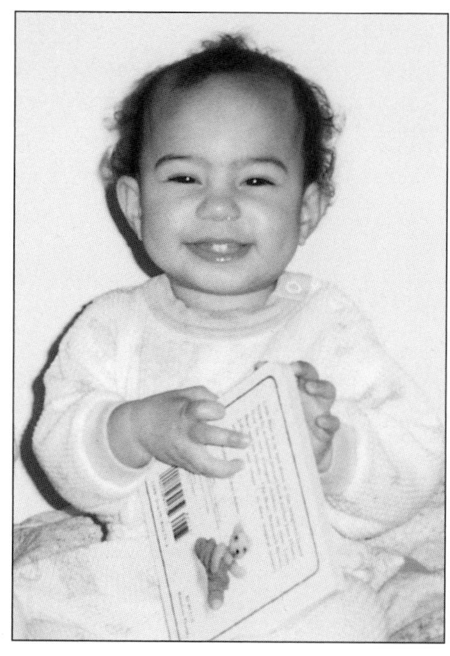

In the daily routine of life, point out and read print in the environment —such as words on a restaurant menu, labels on food containers, posters on a bus, and signs out on the street. Remember that, at early ages, children may not notice that what you are reading is the letters, not the entire sign or label. Help them notice how important small differences in the letters and words are, even when the general label or sign is the same. For example, when they pay attention to a product like ice cream with a favorite logo, help them notice the differences in flavors indicated by words on the label.

Label some of the important things in the child's universe. To make it fun, explain what you are doing and get the child involved in making artwork on labels for items like videos, books, and art supplies. Be sure to put up some signs that use the child's name, for example, "Marie's Room," "Sam's Treasure Box." Have the child decorate the sign.

Learning About Print

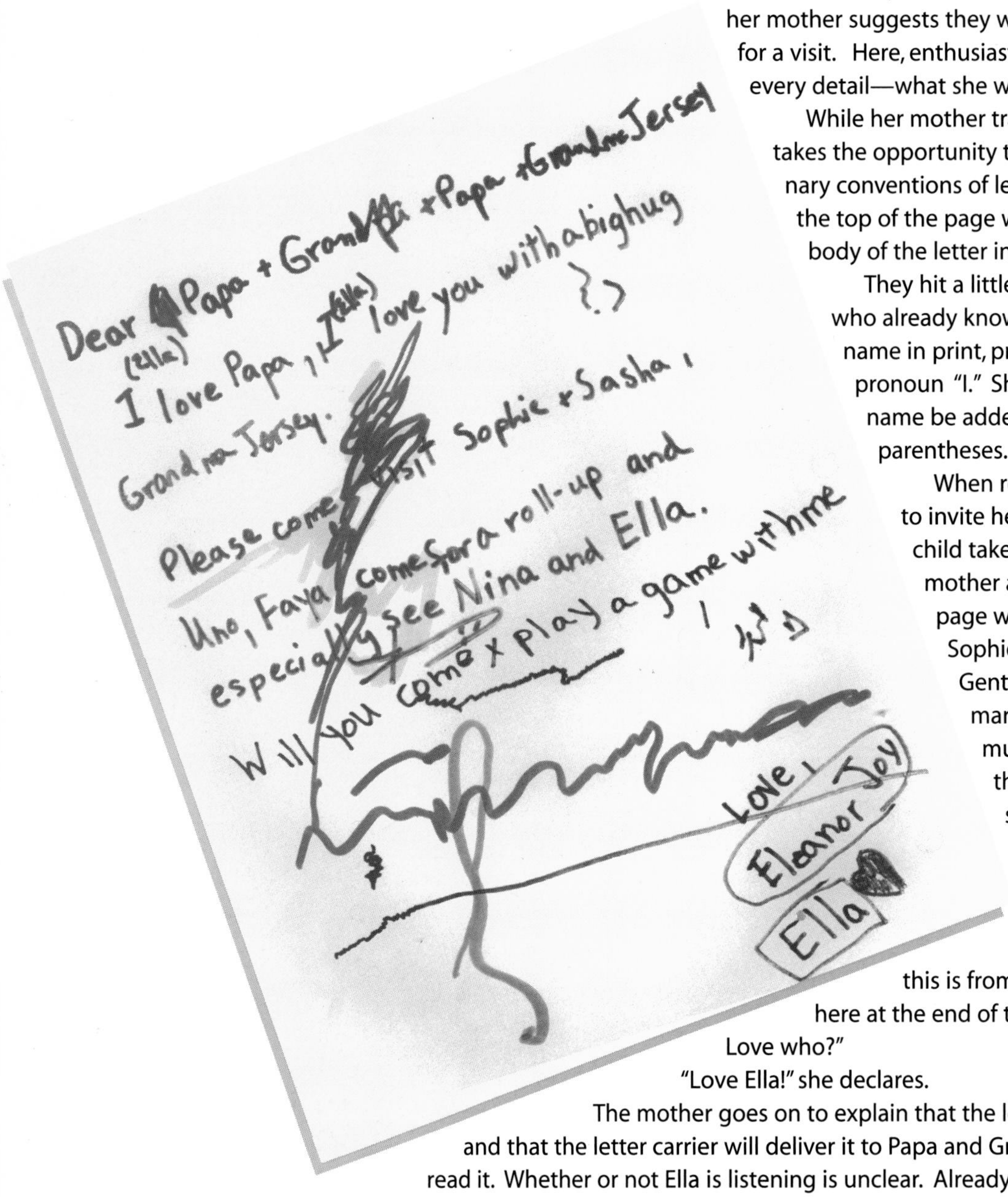
Dear Papa + Grandma + Papa + Grandma Jersey
I love Papa, I (Ella) love you with a big hug
(Ella)
Grandma Jersey.
Please come visit Sophie + Sasha,
Uno, Faya come for a roll-up and
especially see Nina and Ella.
Will you come + play a game with me
Love,
Eleanor Joy
Ella

When three-year-old Ella misses her grandparents, her mother suggests they write a letter and invite them for a visit. Here, enthusiastic Ella dictates—down to every detail—what she wants to say.

While her mother transcribes Ella's words, she takes the opportunity to demonstrate some ordinary conventions of letter writing, like starting at the top of the page with "Dear" and writing the body of the letter in the middle.

They hit a little stumbling block when Ella, who already knows how to recognize her own name in print, protests when she sees the pronoun "I." She insists that her actual name be added. Her mother does so in parentheses.

When reminded that her purpose is to invite her grandparents for a visit, the child takes the marker away from her mother and makes scribbles on the page while saying, "Please come visit Sophie and Sasha" (her pets).

Gently, the mother takes back the marker and explains that she must write words in order for the grandparents to understand. After this, Ella dictates all they will do on their visit, such as play a game and eat a fruit roll-up.

"Now we have to say that this is from you. We write that down here at the end of the letter. We write Love. Love who?"

"Love Ella!" she declares.

The mother goes on to explain that the letter will go to the post office and that the letter carrier will deliver it to Papa and Grandma's house so they can read it. Whether or not Ella is listening is unclear. Already she is off to the next thing, picking up a doll, beginning a game of pretend.

I C
B Y
Q E Z
C S O H N

Functions of Print

Children need to understand that print is meaningful in their daily lives and has many functions. For example, young children can learn that print gives us information—such as directions to a friend's house, how to bake a cake. They can learn that print helps us solve problems, like written instructions for assembling a toy.

Through exposure to a wide array of books, children learn that print can entertain us, amuse us, and even comfort us. Through experiences with "writing," children learn to distinguish between drawing and writing. Their scribbling becomes more purposeful, and as older toddlers they make some scribbles that, to their total joy, look somewhat like English writing. In the preschool years they can be encouraged to write (scribble) messages as part of playful activity.

Activities

Show children how different sorts of written and printed materials work and give them a chance to imitate. For example, when ordinary texts come into the house—bills, mail, take-out menus, announcements—share some of them with children, pointing out what the print is intended to do. "Now I know that you are having a party at school next week," a parent might explain, after reading a flyer from preschool. Similarly, the day-care teacher can talk with children about flyers and notes being sent home with the children.

When jotting down a shopping list or leaving a note on the table or bulletin board for a family member or another staff person, occasionally explain to the child why you are doing it and what it says. Make writing materials available so that children have the chance to write (or scribble) pretend items like lists, letters, and menus themselves.

Make a point of looking up answers to questions. For example, when deciding what to wear for the day, you and your child can find out what the weather will be by reading the newspaper. "Cold and windy, chance of snow," reads one father aloud. "We'd better put on our coats today." When several of the preschoolers are arguing about what kind of dog they saw outside the playground, a teacher can use a book to settle the question.

Key Aspects of Language and Literacy, **Birth to Age Four**

Print Concepts

Adults sometimes forget that children have to learn the most basic conventions that govern written language, such as the spaces that separate the words. The words of English text run from left to right and from top to bottom. That means that a sentence starts at the upper left of a page and continues from left to right. At the end of the line, the sentence continues until the punctuation indicates the end of one sentence and the beginning of the next. i

Activities

During regular reading and writing sessions, adults can explain how print works. For example, before reading a book, look at the cover and read the title and author's name. While reading the book itself, occasionally run your finger along the text so children can discover that text is read from left to right.

When you need to take a break from reading, for example to answer a question, use the opportunity to point out something that experienced readers take for granted—that there are stops built into text. Say to the child, "Let me finish this sentence before I answer that question." Then point to the period when you get there. "There—that's the end of the sentence. Okay, now let's see if we can figure out your question." This helps children learn one aspect of how print works—that there are parts to it, such as sentences, paragraphs, and chapters, and that the end of a line or a page is not necessarily the end of a unit of meaning.

Letter and Early Word Recognition

Preschool-age children can begin to recognize some printed alphabet letters and words, especially the ones in their own names. Many children learn the names of the letters first by singing the alphabet song or reciting them to pushes on the swing. At three and four they begin to attach the names of letters to their shapes. With help, they may soon begin to attend to beginning letters in words that they are familiar with in printed form.

Activities

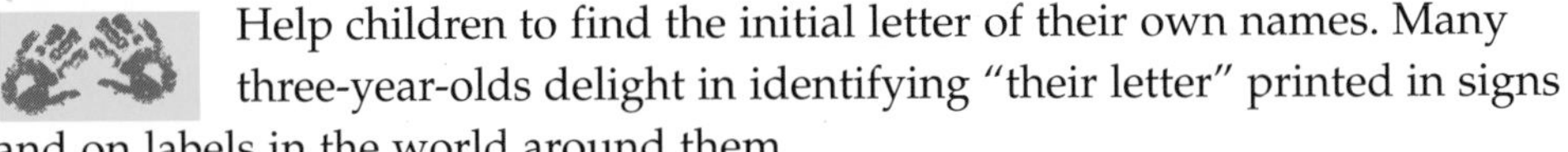

Help children to find the initial letter of their own names. Many three-year-olds delight in identifying "their letter" printed in signs and on labels in the world around them.

Write, display, and point out the child's name often. Print it on their artwork and help them recognize it. As children get older, help them learn to recognize additional words they frequently see printed in the world around them: for example, a word on a favorite t-shirt, "STOP" in stop signs, and other favorites such as "zoo," "mom," and "dad."

Watch TV programs such as Sesame Street with your child and learn the letter songs with them.

The Most Important Letter

Three-year-old Cara has just discovered the first letter in her name and suddenly she is in a world of "Cs." Walking around the house, clutching the letter "C" from her alphabet block set, she is on the lookout. "Hey, there's my C," she cries pointing to a tin of cocoa in the kitchen. She notices the letter again, when she and her babysitter are reading a book about cats. Later that day, while riding on the bus, she looks out the window and calls out excitedly, "There's my letter!" while passing by a large neon sign for Carl's Restaurant. "There's my C!"

Comprehension

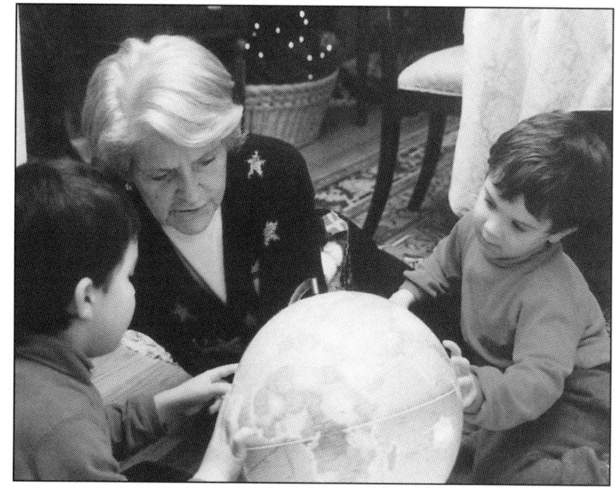

As children move from toddlerhood to school age, they should increasingly be able to grasp the meaning of language they hear spoken in everyday conversation, as well as in narrative forms, such as books. They show this understanding through their questions and comments. When reading a story, they should freely relate information and events in the book to real-life experiences. As they get older, they should become comfortable with following who said or did what in a story.

Activities

Listen to an audio recording of a book on tape. This can be done while looking at the accompanying book or listening to the tape alone. Then have the children draw a picture of their favorite part of the story and talk with them about it. i

While reading a book together, ask children questions to help them think about or reflect on vocabulary words, the plot, or something about a character.

Key Aspects of
Language and Literacy,
Birth to Age Four

Storytime Questions

At a storytime reading session, a librarian reads The Paper Bag Princess. *At various points during the reading, she stops and asks questions to make sure that children understand. Anyone reading with a child can follow her technique.*

After getting the children settled in a circle, the librarian holds up the cover of the book and reads the title. Then she points to the picture of a dragon on the cover. "Children, this is a dragon. Do you know what a dragon is?"

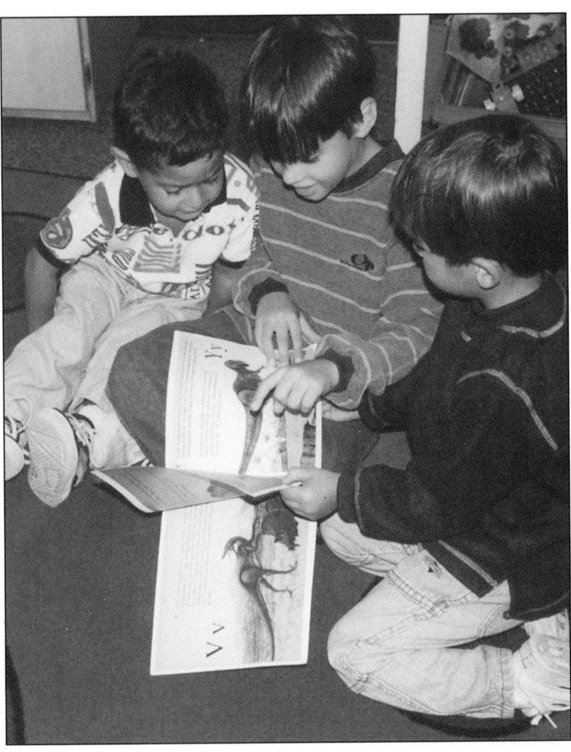

"A dragon is a monster!" answers one child.

"A dragon is big and scary!" replies another.

"A dragon is pretend!" replies another.

After several similar responses, the librarian gives an encouraging, "Yes! exactly. A dragon is a big scary creature. It has wings, and some dragons can even breathe fire from their mouths, and it is pretend."

She then proceeds to read the story. As the plot unfolds, she pauses in her reading and asks questions to help the children predict what is coming next. "What do you think the prince is going to say to the paper bag princess?" she asks and waits patiently while several children put forth wildly different answers. "Well, let's see if we got it," she says, then moves forward.

Later, to help children with their understanding of the main character, she asks, "Why do you think the princess is getting the dragon to show how strong he is?"

With these sorts of questions, the reader helps ensure that children understand the text. But the questions also have another purpose: to help children learn how to think about literature and how to look for what is important in a story or any piece of text.

Literacy as a Source of Enjoyment

Children need to feel positive about reading and literacy experiences. They often make displays of reading or writing attempts, calling attention to themselves: "Look at my story." And the adults around should take time to find out about the child's work.

Activities

Create a warm atmosphere around storytime, reading, and pretend play activities. Once in a while, invite other favorite people to join in during reading time. Respond to children's remarks and observations about books, and take time to answer their questions while reading. Make literacy activities fun and a part of play—events they look forward to, rather than those they feel forced into. Give them a chance to choose the books they want to read, but you should choose a few too—both to make sure that you have some manageable selections in the pile you bring home and to let them see you participate in the fun of the choosing.

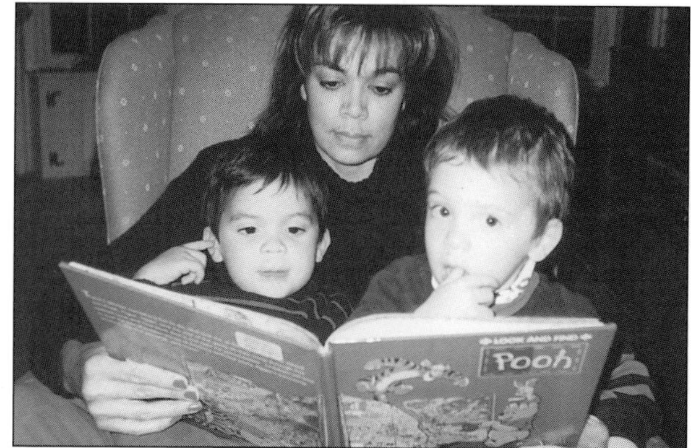

Take children to the library regularly, and remember to offer them many kinds of books. One child may dislike all storybooks, but fall in love with nonfiction books about dinosaurs, trains, animals, or nature. Other children love nursery rhymes and poetry. All young children will want you to read favorite books again and again, but four- and five-year-olds will also develop a frequent need for new and different books.

For children who love TV, videos, and CD-ROMs, connect these visual experiences to reading and books. For example, after watching a nature program about animals, get a book on a similar topic and extend their knowledge and enjoyment. Act out scenes from a favorite video. Or create homemade books with themes from television shows or videos. Use pictures cut out from magazines or catalogs, the child's drawings, and labels written by an adult to create the child's very own book.

Nourishing the Mind with High-Quality Books

Reading nourishes growing young minds, and children need to have high-quality books in their lives. When taking a child to the library, ask the librarian for suggestions. Tell her your child's age and interests. Be on the lookout look for award-winning literature, such as recipients of the Caldecott, Newberry, and American Library Association awards. Also, check your local paper's book review section.

Many libraries and universities compile lists of all-time great books for kids, such as the following one, put together by the New York Public Library (available on the Internet at www.nypl.org/branch/kids/gloria.html). Similar lists are compiled and available from the Boulder Public Library (bcn.boulder.co.us/library/bpl/child/topclis.html) and Great Book Stuff (www.kels.org/webkids/grbkstuf.html).

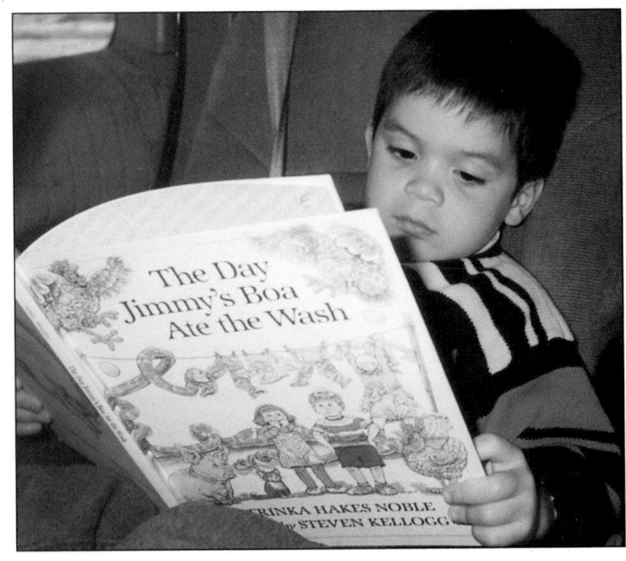

100 Great Picture Books

Compiled by the New York Public Library

Abuela by Arthur Dorros. Illustrated by Elisa Kleven. Dutton.

Alexander and the Terrible, Horrible, No Good, Very Bad Day by Judith Viorst. Illustrated by Ray Cruz. Atheneum.

Animals Should Definitely Not Wear Clothing by Judi Barrett. Illustrated by Ron Barrett. Atheneum.

Anansi and the Moss-Covered Rock by Eric A. Kimmel. Illustrated by Janet Stevens. Holiday House.

Andy and the Lion by Juan Daugherty. Viking.

Ben's Trumpet by Rachel Isadora. Greenwillow.

Blueberries for Sal by Robert McCloskey. Viking.

The Bossy Gallito: A Traditional Cuban Folk Tale retold by Lucia M. Gonzalez. Illustrated by Lulu Delacre. Scholastic.

Bread and Jam for Frances by Russell Hoban. Illustrated by Lillian Hoban. HarperCollins.

Brown Bear, Brown Bear, What Do You See? by Bill Martin, Jr. Illustrated by Eric Carle. Holt.

Caps for Sale: A Tale of a Peddler, Some Monkeys and Their Monkey Business by Esphyr Slobodkina. HarperCollins.

The Carrot Seed by Ruth Krauss. Illustrated by Crockett Johnson. HarperCollins.

A Chair for My Mother by Vera B. Williams. Greenwillow.

Chicka Chicka Boom Boom by Bill Martin, Jr., and John Archambault. Illustrated by Lois Ehlert. Simon & Schuster.

Corduroy by Don Freeman. Viking.

Curious George by H.A. Rey. Houghton.

The Day Jimmy's Boa Ate the Wash by Trinka H. Noble. Illustrated by Steven Kellogg. Dial.

Dear Zoo by Rod Campbell. Simon & Schuster.

Doctor De Soto by William Steig. Farrar.

Farmer Duck by Martin Waddell. Illustrated by Helen Oxenbery. Candlewick Press.

The Fortune-Tellers by Lloyd Alexander. Illustrated by Trina Schart Hyman. Dutton.

Freight Train by Donald Crews. Greenwillow.

George and Martha by James Marshall. Houghton.

Go Away, Big Green Monster! by Ed Emberley. Little, Brown.

Good Night, Gorilla by Peggy Rathmann. Putnam.

Goodnight Moon by Margaret W. Brown. Illustrated by Clement Hurd. HarperCollins.

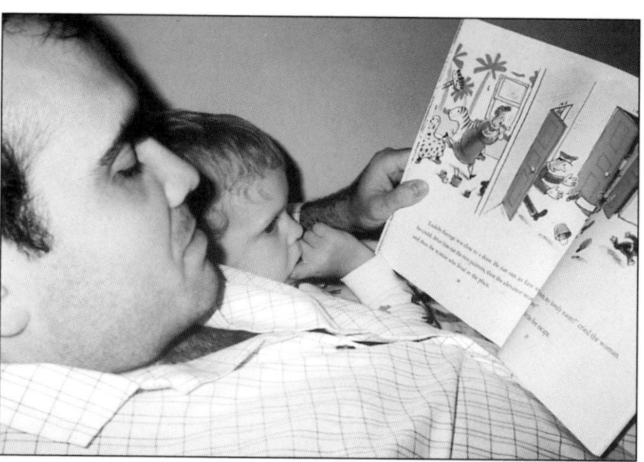

Grandfather's Journey by Allen Say. Houghton.

Happy Birthday, Moon by Frank Asch. Simon & Schuster.

Harold and the Purple Crayon by Crockett Johnson. HarperCollins.

Harry the Dirty Dog by Gene Zion. Illustrated by Margaret Graham. HarperCollins.

Henny Penny illustrated by Paul Galdone. Clarion.

Horton Hatches the Egg by Dr. Seuss. Random House.

I Know an Old Lady Who Swallowed a Fly illustrated by Glen Rounds. Holiday House.

If You Give a Mouse a Cookie by Laura J. Numeroff. Illustrated by Felicia Bond. HarperCollins.

Is It Red? Is It Yellow? Is It Blue? An Adventure in Color by Tana Hoban. Greenwillow.

It Could Always Be Worse: A Yiddish Folktale retold and illustrated by Margot Zemach. Farrar.

John Henry by Julius Lester. Illustrated by Jerry Pinkney. Dial.

The Judge: An Untrue Tale by Harve Zemach. Illustrated by Margot Zemach. Viking.

Julius by Angela Johnson. Illustrated by Dav Pilkey. Orchard.

Komodo! by Peter Sís. Greenwillow.

Leo the Late Bloomer by Robert Kraus. Illustrated by Jose Aruego. HarperCollins.

Little Blue and Little Yellow by Leo Lionni. Astor-Honor.

The Little Dog Laughed and Other Nursery Rhymes by Lucy Cousins. Dutton.

The Little Old Lady Who Was Not Afraid of Anything by Linda Williams. Illustrated by Megan Lloyd. HarperCollins.

Little Red Riding Hood retold and illustrated by Paul Galdone. McGraw-Hill.

Lunch by Denise Fleming. Holt.

Lyle, Lyle, Crocodile by Bernard Waber. Houghton.

Madeline by Ludwig Bemelmans. Viking.

Maisie Goes Swimming by Lucy Cousins. Little, Brown.

Make Way for Ducklings by Robert McCloskey. Viking.

Martha Calling by Susan Meddaugh. Houghton.

Mike Mulligan and His Steam Shovel by Virginia L. Burton. Houghton.

Millions of Cats by Wanda Gág. Putnam.

Miss Nelson Is Missing by Harry Allard and James Marshall. Illustrated by James Marshall. Houghton.

Mr. Gumpy's Outing by John Burningham. Holt.

The Monkey and the Crocodile retold and illustrated by Paul Galdone. Clarion.

Morris' Disappearing Bag by Rosemary Wells. Dial.

Mouse Paint by Ellen S. Walsh. Harcourt.

Mufaro's Beautiful Daughters: An African Tale retold and illustrated by John Steptoe. Lothrop.

Mushroom in the Rain adapted from the Russian of V. Suteyev by Mirra Ginsburg. Illustrated by Jose Aruego and Ariane Dewey. Simon & Schuster.

The Napping House by Audrey Wood. Illustrated by Don Wood. Harcourt.

Officer Buckle and Gloria by Peggy Rathmann. Putnam.

Old Black Fly by Jim Aylesworth. Illustrated by Stephen Gammell. Holt.

Over in the Meadow by John Langstaff. Illustrated by Feodor Rojankovsky. Harcourt.

Owen by Kevin Henkes. Greenwillow.

Papa, Please Get the Moon for Me by Eric Carle. Simon & Schuster.

Perez and Martina by Pura Belpré. Illustrated by Carlos Sanchez. Viking.

Pierre: A Cautionary Tale by Maurice Sendak. HarperCollins.

The Polar Express by Chris Van Allsburg. Houghton.

The Random House Book of Mother Goose: A Treasury of 386 Timeless Nursery Rhymes selected and illustrated by Arnold Lobel. Random House.

Rosie's Walk by Pat Hutchins. Simon & Schuster.

Round Trip by Ann Jonas. Greenwillow.

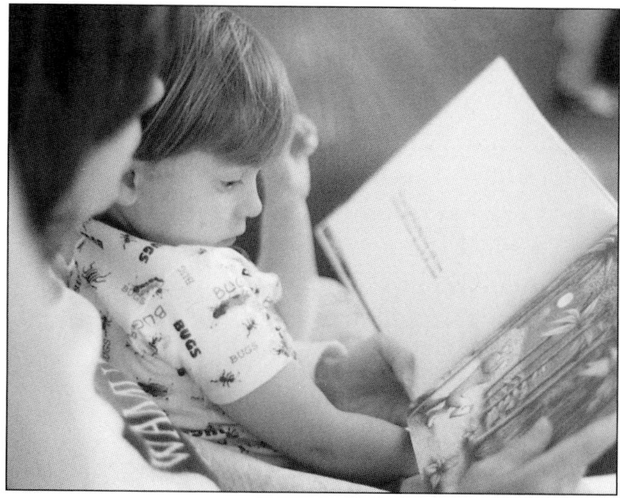

Rumpelstiltskin retold and illustrated by Paul O. Zelinsky. Dutton.

Seven Blind Mice by Ed Young. Putnam.

The Snowy Day by Ezra Jack Keats. Viking.

Stone Soup retold and illustrated by Marcia Brown. Simon & Schuster.

The Story of Babar, the Little Elephant by Jean de Brunhoff. Random House.

The Story of Ferdinand by Munro Leaf. Illustrated by Robert Lawson. Viking.

Strega Nona by Tomie De Paola. Simon & Schuster.

Swamp Angel by Anne Isaacs. Illustrated by Paul O. Zelinsky. Dutton.

Swimmy by Leo Lionni. Knopf.

Sylvester and the Magic Pebble by William Steig. Simon & Schuster.

The Tale of Peter Rabbit by Beatrix Potter. Warne.

Ten, Nine, Eight by Molly Bang. Greenwillow.

There's a Nightmare in My Closet by Mercer Mayer. Dial.

The Three Billy Goats Gruff by P.C. Asbjfrnsen and J.E. Moe. Illustrated by Marcia Brown. Harcourt.

The Three Robbers by Tomi Ungerer. Atheneum.

Tikki Tikki Tembo retold by Arlene Mosel. Illustrated by Blair Lent. Holt.

The True Story of the Three Little Pigs by A. Wolf as told to John Scieszka. Illustrated by Lane Smith. Viking.

Tuesday by David Wiesner. Houghton.

Two of Everything: A Chinese Folktale retold and illustrated by Lily Toy Hong. Whitman.

The Very Hungry Caterpillar by Eric Carle. Philomel.

We're Going on a Bear Hunt retold by Michael Rosen. Illustrated by Helen Oxenbury. McElderry.

The Wheels on the Bus adapted and illustrated by Paul O. Zelinsky. Dutton.

When I Was Young in the Mountains by Cynthia Rylant. Illustrated by Diane Goode. Dutton.

Where the Wild Things Are by Maurice Sendak. HarperCollins.

Where's Spot? by Eric Hill. Putnam.

Whistle for Willie by Ezra Jack Keats. Viking.

Why Mosquitoes Buzz in People's Ears: A West African Tale retold by Verna Aardema. Illustrated by Leo and Diane Dillon. Dial.

Zomo the Rabbit: A Trickster Tale from West Africa retold and illustrated by Gerald McDermott. Harcourt.

Literacy—from Parent to Child

Parents can influence their children's literacy by involving them in a wide variety of play and everyday activities that involve language. Talking to toddlers, sharing in making and using grocery lists, singing songs, telling stories—all of this helps children build literacy skills. Another important influence is having a positive attitude about learning. Children whose families communicate that achievement is expected and appreciated tend to do better.

Parents can learn a great deal about their children's learning. For example, they can be on the lookout for potential difficulties and discuss some of their valuable observations with teachers. Starting at age three or four, parents can observe whether or not children remember nursery rhymes and can play rhyming games. At about age four, parents can notice if children have trouble getting information or directions from conversations or texts that are read aloud to them. Once children are in kindergarten, parents should be attuned to whether they are beginning to name the letters and numbers that they see in different contexts and to write them. Five-year-olds should also be happy and able to play simple alliterative games, enjoying, for example, "I'm thinking of something that starts with the letter 'b'" as a way to pass the time on longer trips in the car. As a child gets to be five and six, parents can observe whether the child acts as if he or she understands that spoken words can be broken down into smaller parts (for example, noticing "big" in "bigger" and the "egg" in "beg"), and that you can change a small part of a word and it becomes a very different thing (for example, changing initial consonants to make "cat," "hat," "sat"). That said, it is critical that parents always be aware of the tremendous variability among normal, smart children, and that it can be difficult to measure progress.

Talking to a Baby: Day Care Environments

Babysitters and day care providers have an important—and growing—responsibility for children's early literacy and reading development. They must understand that oral language is fundamental to reading, and they should have frequent one-to-one conversation with babies, maintaining eye contact with them. All day care settings should involve singing songs, reciting nursery rhymes, talking to babies in the course of everyday activity, and repeating back to a baby those "ba ba ba's" and "ga ga ga's." As coos and gurgles give way to real words, caregivers should encourage children to talk, repeating what the child is saying and elaborating for the child when appropriate. (Appropriate language and literacy activities for very young children are featured earlier in this book. See pages 19-37.)

"We don't drill toddlers with their ABCs. Instead, we create a language-rich environment. We have circle time, when we sing songs and use hand gestures to accompany the words. When I read The Three Little Bears, *I don't just tell stories. I'll show them three stuffed animals. I'll find three chairs. When the kids do begin to speak, I try to figure out what they're saying and repeat it back—even if it's not entirely comprehensible. I help them understand that language has a lot of power and they can get what they want by using language."*

—Scott Hirose
Teacher/therapist
Queens Child Guidance Center
Therapeutic nursery for children age 0 to 3
Jamaica, New York

High-Quality Preschool

High-quality preschool programs can boost language and literacy skills and, ultimately, reading achievement. But quality is essential, and many preschools fall short in promoting language and literacy.

In a high-quality preschool, the teacher should provide a good model of verbal language throughout the day. For example, when a child points a finger and says "Dat," the teacher has a number of good choices. She could expand for him and say, "You want the red ball?" or she could say, gently, "Tell me what you want," or "Tell me what you want in words." Some teachers say, "Use your words" but accept the closest approximation that they think the child can produce. She should also have informal conversations with each child every day, encouraging them to use language by asking open-ended questions, such as *why*, *how*, and *what-if*.

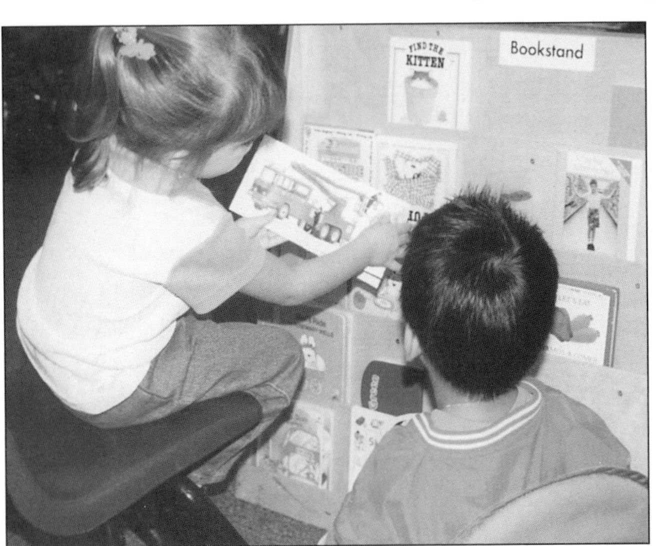

Preschools should help children to learn, think, and talk about new domains of knowledge. They do this by providing opportunities for children to use language in a variety of ways, by ensuring lots of interesting conversations in which children are involved, by offering opportunity to play with language in ways that support phonological awareness and by incorporating meaningful uses of literacy into everyday activities. Children who have a wide body of background knowledge and life experiences are more likely to succeed in reading. They are more likely to relate to stories, recognize words in them, and to understand events described in books.

Children in America need more opportunities to attend affordable preschools where they will experience high-quality language and literacy environments. If we are to prevent reading difficulties, then children must start school motivated to learn and with the language skills they need in order to learn.

All too often preschool and day care settings for young children provide poor language and literacy environments—particularly for those whose families have limited resources. It is critical that these settings be designed to support language and literacy. As part of this effort, parents, teachers, pediatricians, social workers, speech language therapists, and other preschool practitioners should strive, using research-derived guidelines, to help children overcome language problems as early as possible.

Excellence Makes the Difference

How much of an impact can preschool make in a child's life?

An excellent preschool program can give children long-term benefits that follow them into adulthood. That's what one study found when researchers tracked children from early childhood through high school and beyond. In this important study, data revealed that children in an excellent part-day preschool program had less need for special education, less grade retention, and significantly higher high school graduation rates than children who did not attend a good preschool. i

What accounted for this particular program's success? Some of the essential features included:

A well-supplied, well-designed preschool space. The room was divided into various interest areas (e.g., water play, drawing and painting, music, pretend play, reading, and writing).

A regular daily routine. By providing regular expectations and schedules for classroom routines such as planning time, work time, clean-up time, small-group time, outside time, and circle time, children learn to conduct themselves in each activity and when and how to transition between them.

Strong parent-teacher communication: Teachers had regular communication with parents, including home visits.

Strong teaching methods and teamwork among teachers. Teachers gave children a comfortable, secure environment that promoted active learning. They encouraged and supported children's actions and language. They helped children make choices and decisions and helped them solve their own problems and do things for themselves. Each day, teachers recorded and shared with other teachers notes on each child's activities and progress.

A varied curriculum. The curriculum promoted children's learning in many domains, such as creative representations (pretend play, model-making, drawing, and painting); language and literacy; initiative-taking

and social relations; movement; music; classification and seriation (arranging objects in order or patterns—such as color and size—and describing their relationship, such as biggest to smallest); numbers (counting and relationships—such as more, fewer, the same); space (experiencing and describing position, direction, and distances in the classroom, the building, and neighborhood); and time (concept of time and sequence of events).

Language experiences. Adults regularly engaged children in conversation, soliciting their responses and focusing on their strengths. They talked with children about personally meaningful experiences, describing objects and events.

Literacy experiences. Adults encouraged writing experiences (such as drawing, scribbling, and invented spelling), and reading (such as reading storybooks, signs, symbols, and one's own writing).

Language and Literacy Activities in Preschool

Earlier in this chapter, *Growing Up to Read*, we presented language and literacy activities for adults and children in a variety of informal settings. In this current section we present activities for the preschool. As with the first set of activities, our main purpose is to illustrate the underlying concepts important for preparing children for reading instruction. We expect that the individual activities included will be helpful for most children; however, they are examples rather than comprehensive curricula in themselves. i

Phonological Awareness

As mentioned earlier in this book, phonological awareness involves an appreciation of the sounds, as well as the meanings, of spoken words. A child who is phonologically aware can demonstrate this, for example: by perceiving and producing rhymes (fan, tan, man, etc.); by dividing words up into their syllables (hel/i/cop/ter) and smaller components (sn/ake), and putting them back together; by noticing that groups of words have the same beginning (star, story), middle (bag, cat) or ending (pinch, lunch). Recent research has confirmed that children who have a greater degree of phonological awareness when they enter school are better equipped to learn to read.

A more advanced form of phonological awareness, called phonemic awareness, is the understanding that speech can be broken down into even smaller units (phonemes). This is very important for learning to read, because phonemes are what letters usually stand for. (The idea that letters, or groups of letters, represent phonemes is called the alphabetic principle.) For example, the word "book" is made up of three phonemes, represented in writing by "b," "oo," and "k." Few preschoolers spontaneously attain phonemic awareness, but many studies have shown that they can acquire this understanding by engaging in activities that draw their attention to the existence of phonemes in spoken words. i

Preschool teachers can use many appropriate activities to help build phonological awareness in young preschoolers and phonemic awareness in older children. Rhyming songs, syllable-clapping, and grouping objects according to how their names begin can all be used to draw children's attention to the sounds of speech. Later, to promote phonemic awareness, the activities can include:

- isolating the first segment of a word (Say the first little bit of "snake");
- finding all the objects on a poster that begin with the "nnn" sound;

- discovering what is left when a particular segment is removed from a word (e.g., Say "smile" without the "sss." Say "team" without the "mmm");
- breaking one-syllable words into their phonemes; and
- blending phonemes to make a word (What word does "mmm...ooo...nnn" make?).

Commercial products (books, software) for preschool teachers, with games involving these kinds of activities, are becoming more and more available. Talking about phonemes can also be integrated with letter learning, so that children can be introduced to the sounds of letters (i.e., the phonemes that they stand for) as well as to their names.

Activities

Children should play with sound and rhymes through a variety of games and songs. Examples of these games and songs follow

Sing songs that play with sound 

I Can Hear the Rain

Pitter patter, pitter patter, I can hear the rain.

Pitter patter, pitter patter, I can hear the rain.

OO, OO, I can hear the wind.

OO, OO, I can hear the wind.

Language and Literacy Activities in Preschool

Sing songs that play with rhyme 

This Old Man

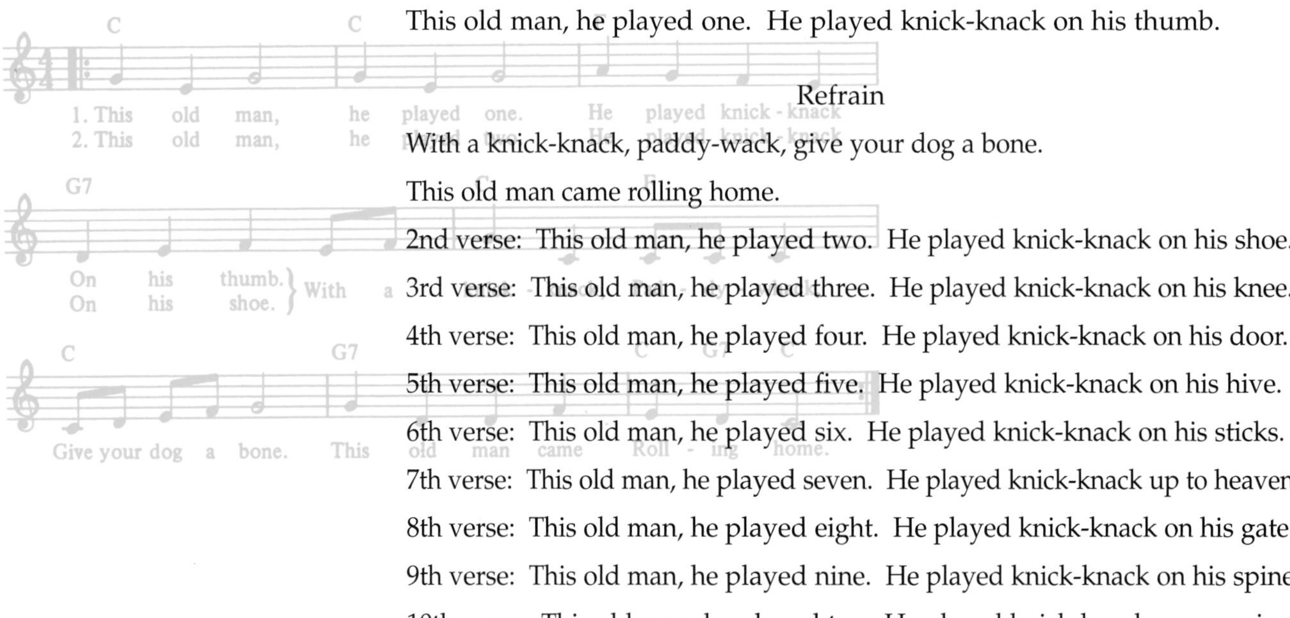

This old man, he played one. He played knick-knack on his thumb.

Refrain

With a knick-knack, paddy-wack, give your dog a bone.

This old man came rolling home.

2nd verse: This old man, he played two. He played knick-knack on his shoe.

3rd verse: This old man, he played three. He played knick-knack on his knee.

4th verse: This old man, he played four. He played knick-knack on his door.

5th verse: This old man, he played five. He played knick-knack on his hive.

6th verse: This old man, he played six. He played knick-knack on his sticks.

7th verse: This old man, he played seven. He played knick-knack up to heaven.

8th verse: This old man, he played eight. He played knick-knack on his gate.

9th verse: This old man, he played nine. He played knick-knack on his spine.

10th verse: This old man, he played ten. He played knick-knack once again.

Read rhyming poetry and rhyming stories

The Spider

I'm told that the spider
Has coiled up inside her
Enough silky material
To spin an aerial
One-way track
to the moon and back;
Whilst I
Cannot even catch a fly.

Sociodramatic Play
Through teacher and peer interactions in sociodramatic play, children use new language as they plan, negotiate, compose, and carry out the "script" of their play. In addition, they practice verbal and narrative skills that are important to the development of reading comprehension.

Activities

Every preschool classroom should have special materials and play areas geared toward encouraging children in particular domains while appealing to their interests. Such play centers might include an art center, a nature center, a puppet center, and real-world play areas, such as a store or a restaurant.

These areas should be stocked with writing supplies and printed materials that can be incorporated into play. For example, in a block area, maps and labeled photos of buildings and construction sites could be provided. In a toy area, use some originally labeled toy containers for storage. In a woodworking area, add tool catalogs, home repair magazines, and picture reference books about building. In a house area, include food packaging, menus, appliance instructions, plane tickets, travel brochures, and computer keyboards. In the outdoor area, provide colored chalk, gardening books, and bird and tree guides.

Listening

Integral to speech discrimination and phonological awareness is the basic ability to listen carefully.

Activities

Teachers can have children listen to books on tape in small groups or one at a time. Teachers can organize play activities, songs, and dances that involve listening to directions. Simon Says is an old favorite and can include sequences of directions at one time, once the children learn the basic game.

Oral Language

Through interesting conversations with teachers and peers, children learn vocabulary and language structures that will later help with reading. The key is to prepare for content that is rich and important to the children.

Activities

Make time each day for individual conversations with children. Give each child your full attention during the discussion and be

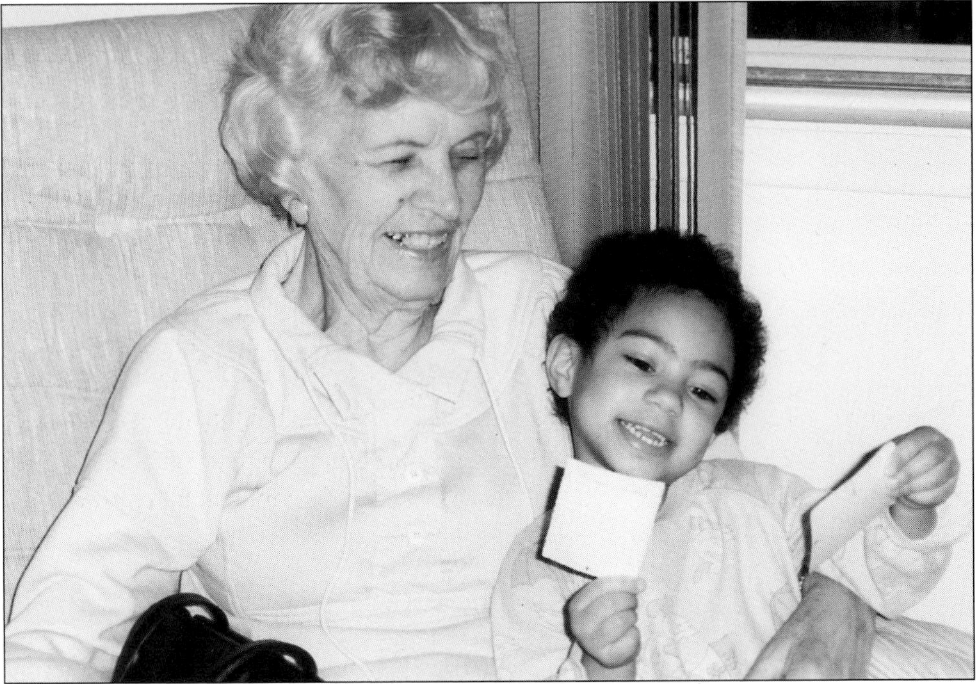

sure to spend enough time listening to what he or she has to say. Give the child the chance to take the conversational lead. Add your own brief responses and comments to draw him or her out. Although they may not always be factually accurate in their responses, it is important for children to learn how to use language to express and describe their impressions and ideas.

Encourage conversation when children are in a comfortable setting. They're more likely to open up and talk when they are in a nonthreatening situation, such as a one-to-one reading session, a walk outside, and during snack time. Perhaps the most effective way to converse with children is to take time to join in their play.

Make a Personal Experiences Center in the classroom, where young children can talk with teachers about events in their lives while the teachers listen, prompt discussion, and record the experiences. Tell children personal stories. Talk about things that interest you. Acknowledge uncertainty about some things, and show children how you find answers to your questions.

Use readings of high-quality storybooks to lead children to reenactments and discussions during class. Have a child dictate his or her own story—"You tell me the story and I'll write the words"—and then act out the story, including other children in the performance.

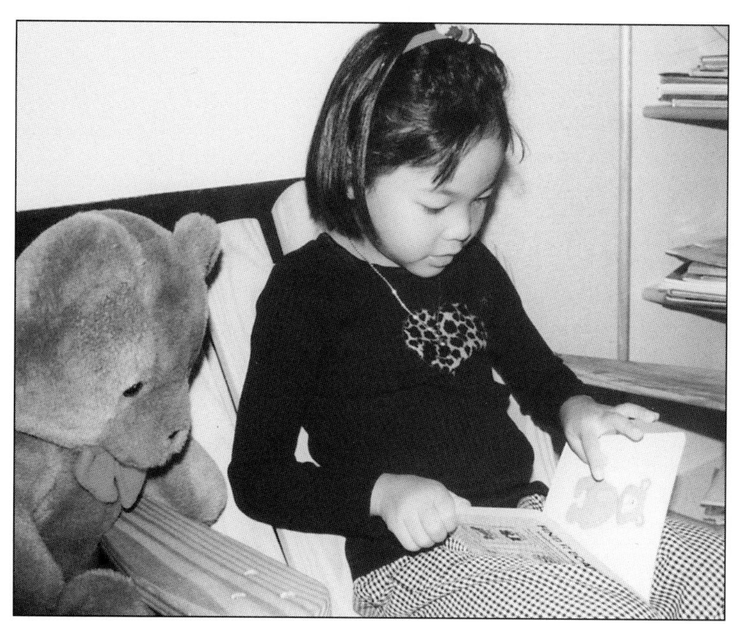

In story dictation, the teacher should move from taking verbatim dictation to asking the child questions about sequences that are unclear—like "Where did the ogre come from?"—and edit accordingly. Many teachers dramatize children's stories and edit when the children recognize that something is missing.

Encourage children to write their own story. Tell them, "It doesn't have to be like grown-up writing, use your own kid writing." Encourage them to "read" it when they are done. Videotape them "reading" their stories from this emergent writing.

Shared Reading

Through teacher-child readings of books, young children learn many of the key aspects of literacy such as book and print awareness, functions of print, and listening comprehension.

Activities

With storybooks or big books, children should have shared reading experiences each and every day. The teacher must not only read out loud, but develop routine practices that will actively engage the children.

Reading With Preschoolers

In addition to reading books to preschoolers while they listen, it is important to discuss the books with them. One program successfully taught child care providers and their parents a systematic way to discuss books.

This method employs (1) a way of interacting with preschoolers while discussing books—called the PEER sequence—and (2) five types of prompts to use during the interactions—called CROWD. The PEER sequence and the CROWD principles always operate within the larger principles of following the child's interests, expecting slightly more of the child each time through the book, and keeping interactions light and fun.

In the PEER sequence:

- P Parent (or other adult) initiates an exchange about the book, and
- E Evaluates the child's response,
- E Expands the child's response, and
- R Repeats the initial question to check that the child understands the new learning.

For example, reading A Mother for Choco:

Adult: "What is Mrs. Bear doing?" (Wh-prompt. See below)
Child: "Standing on her toes."
Adult: "Yes, she's standing on her toes and picking apples." (Evaluates and expands)
Adult (Next time through the book): "What is Mrs. Bear doing? Do you remember? (Repeats question)
Child: "She's standing on her toes and picking apples."
Adult: "That's right, and she's putting them in her basket." (Evaluates and expands)

The CROWD questions* include:

- C Completion questions about the structure of language used in the book, for example, "When Choco talked with the Penguin, he cried 'you have ______ (wings) just like me!'" The child fills in the blank.
- R Recall questions relate to the story content of the book, for example, "Do you remember how this book ended for Choco?"
- O Open-ended questions to increase the amount of talk about a book and to focus on the details of the book, for example, "What is happening on this page?"
- W "Wh" questions to teach new vocabulary, for example, "No matter where Choco searched, he couldn't find a mother who looked just like him. What is a 'search'?"
- D Distancing questions that help the child bridge the material in the book to their real-life experiences, for example, "Does everyone in your family look the same? How do you think Choco felt about everyone in his family looking different?"

* The crowd questions are for older preschoolers. Use only "wh" questions and then open-ended questions for two-year-olds and early three-year-olds.

Exposure to Books

Children need to have high-quality books become a part of their daily experiences.

Activities

The classroom library should be well stocked with a variety of high-quality books and magazines. Children should have the opportunity to select their own books, and the teacher should also suggest books to extend an idea for a classroom activity or to suit an individual child's interest.

Child Care and Literacy

Increasing numbers of very young children are spending time in day care settings, where the main focus has traditionally been on providing good physical care. Literacy enrichment has not been a high priority.

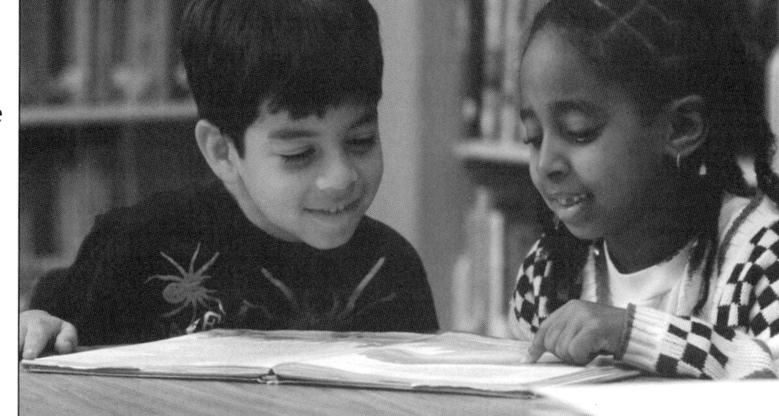

One major obstacle to high-quality day care is the lack of good books in many day care and preschool settings. In one interesting program, a private foundation, a major city library system, and five surrounding county libraries teamed up with a university researcher, early childhood professionals, and day care teachers to bring literacy to the care of children from infancy through age five. The goal: to increase exposure to print and meaningful language among very young children.

In what they called the Great Book Flood of 1996, 322 child care centers serving 17,675 mainly poor children received large quantities of high-quality books—at a ratio of five per child. They also received materials needed to create book areas and library corners. Teachers received 10 hours of training in early literacy development, storybook reading techniques, book selection, and book-related activities. Libraries participated by offering speakers, activities, and celebrations focused on books.

At the end of the program, teachers reported that they read more frequently and for longer periods to their children each day, in addition to giving them greater access to books in the classroom. Children showed substantial benefits, with improvements in their competence at narration, concepts of print, concepts of writing, and letter knowledge. The children continued to show gains at a follow-up study during their kindergarten year.

Letter-Naming

Teachers should help children recognize at least some of the letters of the alphabet. Preschoolers who can recognize and print some letters have an advantage at school entry. Therefore, children should have easy access to letters in many forms: alphabet blocks, letter cards, board games, and ABC's on wall charts at the child's eye height, to name a few.

Activities

Include a number of alphabet books in the library. Share them frequently, inviting the children to name each letter and the pictures on the page that go with it.

Have a Letter of the Day for each of three days in a row. For each letter, decorate a big poster with the uppercase letter in the middle. Ask the children whose first name starts with that letter to come and tape their name cards to the poster. On the second day, compare the posters from the two days. On the third day, compare all three posters. Have all the children find the

From a Well-Known Book on Beginning Reading

G C G C

G C G C

When challenged to name these two letters ("C" and "G"), my daughter, now just three years old, looked me squarely in the eye and said firmly, "I call them both 'C.'" It is not that she could not discriminate their shapes: she regularly performs perfectly on an uppercase letter-matching game on the computer. Nor is she unaware that I like to call these letters by different names: her answer was clearly intended to preempt the correction that she knew I would produce.

But she has a point. In what reasonable kind of world would people agree to call a dachshund and a St. Bernard "dogs" while calling one of these characters a "C" and the other a "G"? To us, the answer is obvious: in the kind of world where people use "C's" and "G's" discriminately for reading and writing—which, of course, she does not yet do.

—Marilyn Jager Adams 

letter in their deck of letter cards and organize a treasure hunt to find the letter in other places in the room. Later, make a big version of the letter on the ground outside—have the children line up and march along the letter shape while chanting something rhythmic about the shape. For example, while marching along the letter "B," they might chant, "Down up, around, around." For the last two days of the week, play games with all three letters, encouraging children to see similarities and differences between the letters. Repeat the activity with additional letters. Start with the letters that start the children's names.

When the children are pretending to write, be aware and congratulate them when they start to make letter-like forms. Talk with them about the difference between drawing and writing and, later, between letters and numbers. Encourage them to copy the letters from the wall chart, to sign their drawings, and to label them.

Remind them to use the letters of the day. When they ask you to label a picture or write down a story, let them print some of the letters they know and like.

Ask the children to bring in their favorite letters for show-and-tell. They can be on a t-shirt, in a book, or on a cereal box. Ask the children to talk about what helps them recognize the letter. One child might say, for example, that a lower case "b" looks like a baseball bat with a ball stuck to it.

Writing

Through early writing experiences, young children learn many of the key aspects of literacy such as print awareness and concepts, functions of print, and possibly phonological awareness.

Activities

Children need access to a variety of paper, writing utensils, and materials for bookmaking—glue, tape, stapler, and book covers. A well-equipped art area should offer paper in several sizes and colors, paints, markers, crayons, and colored pencils. You may also wish to set up a separate writing or office area that includes blank books, paper, envelopes, mailing labels, stickers, and stamps. Don't discourage scribbling and pretend writing, but do provide support and encouragement for writing letters. As you do so, expect, gradually, that more letters will be recognizable. As the children learn to form letters and develop phonological awareness, expect, too, that invented spellings will appear. It may take a few years before many conventional spellings come. Some, such as the child's own name and special phrases like "I love you," may appear early and be memorized, but a true appreciation of conventional spelling comes later.

In addition to letting children experiment with writing themselves, make time to write down their personal dictations. Read back *exactly* what the child said, without correcting grammar or word choices. This shows that you value the child's work and helps children begin to understand the connection between spoken and written language. If a child dictates in a language you do not understand, get the help of a parent volunteer as a transcriber and translator. Children can also act out their dictated stories.

Computer-Based Literacy

Ideally, classrooms would offer preschoolers access to an easy-to-use word processor, printer, software programs for print concepts, stories on CD-ROM, and interactive programs.

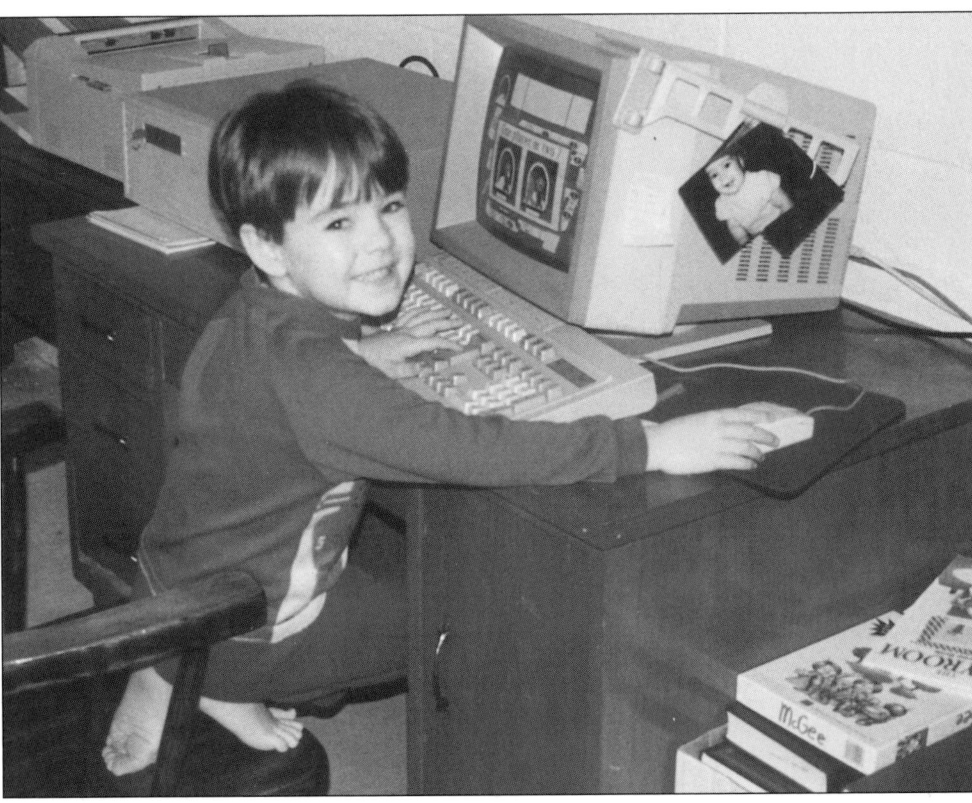

Young Children and Computers

In recent years, the consumer and school markets have become deluged with software products for children—products of dramatically varying quality. Following are three examples of highly rated programs i for three- and four-year-olds. These were rated for content, user friendliness, adult management features, strength of support materials, and value for the cost, rather than being examined for outcomes on children's learning.

Age Group	Program	Brief Description
Three years and older	**Reader Rabbit's Ready for Letters** i	Includes matching, sorting, patterns, letters, and word meanings in five activities. These are Grandma's Kitchen, Mix & Match Bedroom, ABC Bathroom, Picture Parlor, and Grandpa's Workshop.
	Kid Pix i	Easy-to-use graphics and writing creation program. Mouse is used to draw, dribble paint, stamp letters, erase, and create shapes and backgrounds. Keyboard is used for word processing. Children can record their voices along with the drawings and writings.
	Living Books i	These storybooks have approximately 12 pages. The story is presented and each word in the text is highlighted as it is voiced. Each page includes contains 10 to 20 objects that are activated by clicking on them. Examples of stories are Just Grandma and Me, Arthur's Teacher Troubles, Arthur's Reading Race.
Four years and older	**A to Zap** i	An alphabet book of 26 open-ended activities exploring letters, letter names, words, numbers, counting, and other concepts.
	Bailey's Book House i	Children explore alphabet letters and sounds, play with rhyming words, manipulate prepositions, construct stories using preset lists of characters, settings, props, and actions, and create and print their own cards and invitations.
	The Playroom i	Children explore numbers, time, the alphabet, and other learning concepts. In one game, children type words that are shown on the screen. When the word is completed, the program pronounces each phoneme and highlights each letter.

Accomplishments of the Very Young Child

Children engaged in language and literacy activities, observed at home and in preschools, appear mostly playful and exploratory, although in fact they are hard at work as scholars of language and literacy.

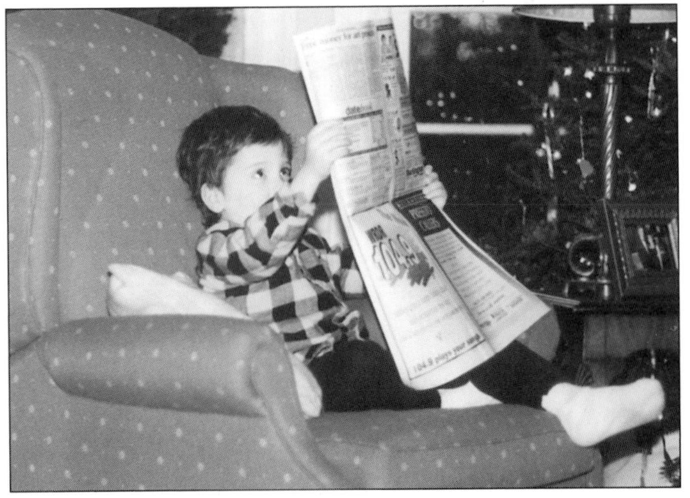

A particular set of accomplishments that the successful learner is likely to exhibit during the preschool years is shown in the table on page 59. Because of their importance, we present them in full, as published in *Preventing Reading Difficulties in Young Children* (National Academy Press, 1998). This list is neither exhaustive nor incontestable, but it does capture many highlights in the course of literacy acquisition that have been revealed through several decades of research. Of course, the timing of these accomplishments will to some extent depend on maturational and experiential differences among children.

Early Childhood Educators

Preschool teachers represent an important—and largely underutilized—resource in promoting literacy through promoting the acquisition of rich language and beginning literacy concepts and skills. Early childhood educators should not try to replicate the formal reading instruction provided in schools; instead, their job is to help children develop the basic knowledge, interest, and understandings that will allow them to flourish once it is time for such instruction. Central to achieving the goal of primary prevention of reading difficulties is the preschool teacher's knowledge base and experience, as well as the support provided to the teacher; each of these may vary according to where the teacher is in his or her professional development.

A critical component in the preparation of teachers before they begin their careers is supervised, relevant, experience in preschools in which they receive ongoing guidance and feedback. A principal goal of this experience is to achieve the ability to integrate and apply the knowledge learned in practice.

Birth to Three-Year-Old Accomplishments

- Recognizes specific books by cover.
- Pretends to read books.
- Understands that books are handled in particular ways.
- Enters into a book-sharing routine with primary caregivers.
- Vocalization play in crib gives way to enjoyment of rhyming language, nonsense word play, etc.
- Labels objects in books.
- Comments on characters in books.
- Looks at picture in book and realizes it is a symbol for real object.
- Listens to stories.
- Requests/commands adult to read or write.
- May begin attending to specific print, such as letters in names.
- Uses increasingly purposeful scribbling.
- Occasionally seems to distinguish between drawing and writing.
- Produces some letter-like forms and scribbles with some features of English writing.

Three- to Four-Year-Old Accomplishments

- Knows that alphabet letters are a special category of visual graphics that can be individually named.
- Recognizes print in the local environment.
- Knows that it is the print that is read in stories.
- Understands that different text forms are used for different functions of print (e.g., a list for groceries is different than the list on a menu).
- Pays attention to separable and repeating sounds in language (e.g., in Peter, Peter, Pumpkin Eater: Peter Eater).
- Uses new vocabulary and grammatical constructions in own speech.
- Understands and follows oral directions.
- Is sensitive to some sequences of events in stories.
- Shows an interest in books and reading.
- When being read a story, connects information and events to real-life experiences.
- Questions and comments demonstrate understanding of literal meaning of story being told.
- Displays reading and writing attempts, calling attention to self: "Look at my story."
- Can identify about 10 alphabet letters, especially those from own name.
- Writes (scribbles) message as part of playful activity.
- May begin to attend to beginning or rhyming sounds in salient words.

Collaborative support by the teacher preparation institution and the field placement is essential.

Programs that educate early childhood professionals should require mastery of information about the many kinds of knowledge and skills that can be acquired in the preschool years in preparation for reading achievement in school. Their knowledge base should include (at least) the following:

- information about how to provide rich conceptual experiences that promote growth in vocabulary and reasoning skills;
- knowledge about word and vocabulary development, from early referential (naming) abilities to relational and abstract terms and finer-shaded meanings;
- knowledge of the early development of speaking and of listening comprehension skills, and the kinds of syntactic and prose structures that preschool children should be in the course of mastering;
- information on young children's sense of story;
- information on young children's sensitivity to the sounds of language;
- information on young children's understanding of concepts of print and the developmental patterns of emergent reading and writing;
- information on young children's development of concepts of space, including directionality;
- knowledge of fine motor development; and
- knowledge about how to instill motivation to read.

Young teachers need support from mentor teachers as they develop. Even after this training is completed, though, teachers need access to ongoing, career-long development.

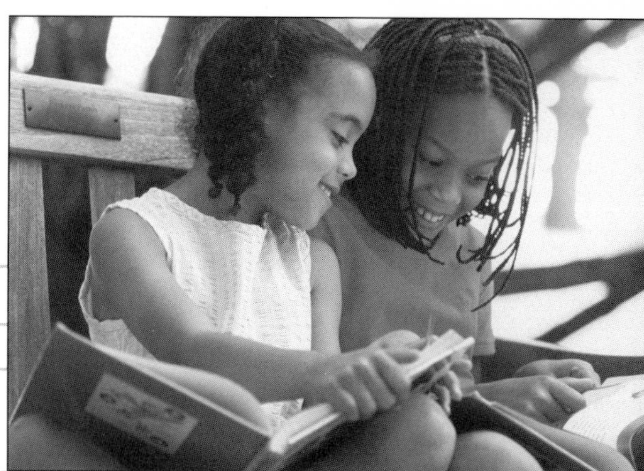

Becoming Real Readers
Kindergarten Through Grade Three

The mission of public schooling is to offer every child full and equal educational opportunity, regardless of the background, education, and income of their parents. To achieve this goal, no time is as precious or as fleeting as the first years of formal schooling. Research consistently shows that children who get off to a good start in reading rarely stumble. Those who fall behind tend to stay behind for the rest of their academic lives.

Supplementary tutoring and remedial instruction can help young readers who are doing poorly. But for all children indeed to have equal educational opportunity, then all children must have excellent curricula—right from the start—in their classrooms, from kindergarten through the primary grades. This chapter provides a view of children learning to read in kindergarten through third grade, using information from the latest research but made concrete through vignettes and activity examples. Our goal is to provide families and communities with a basis for understanding and helping out as teachers work with children who are becoming "real" readers.

Individual Children

In any given classroom in America on any given day, there is a room filled with individual children who are likely to have very different educational strengths and weaknesses. All children simply do not learn everything at the same pace. Children also come to kindergarten and first grade with different kinds of preschool literacy experiences.

Most teachers are given a "scope and sequence" of curriculum skills that they should teach week by week—determined either by their districts or in

High-Quality Teaching: One Classroom

To become real readers, children in kindergarten and the early grades need well-integrated instruction that focuses on three core elements: (1) identifying words using sound-spelling correspondences and sight word recognition, (2) using previous knowledge, vocabulary, and comprehension strategies to read for meaning, and (3) reading with fluency. Good teachers help children master these skills with an engaging variety of activities.

In Mr. Carter's first grade reading class, each student has a personal basket of books, chosen to match his or her abilities and interests. Bulletin boards offer children word attack strategies, with lists of spelling patterns and rhymes. Each child has a journal filled with interesting writing.

Because this is a high-poverty population, the district has made a conscious effort to create small classes. This class has only 18 children—a good thing, considering that the children come from an array of linguistic backgrounds and cultures, including Somalia, the Philippines, Guatemala, and Vietnam.

The room is bright and engaging, with various displays: photos of insects, alphabet letters, days of the week, colors, a tape recorder, and a little horticulture center with seeds and plants growing in the

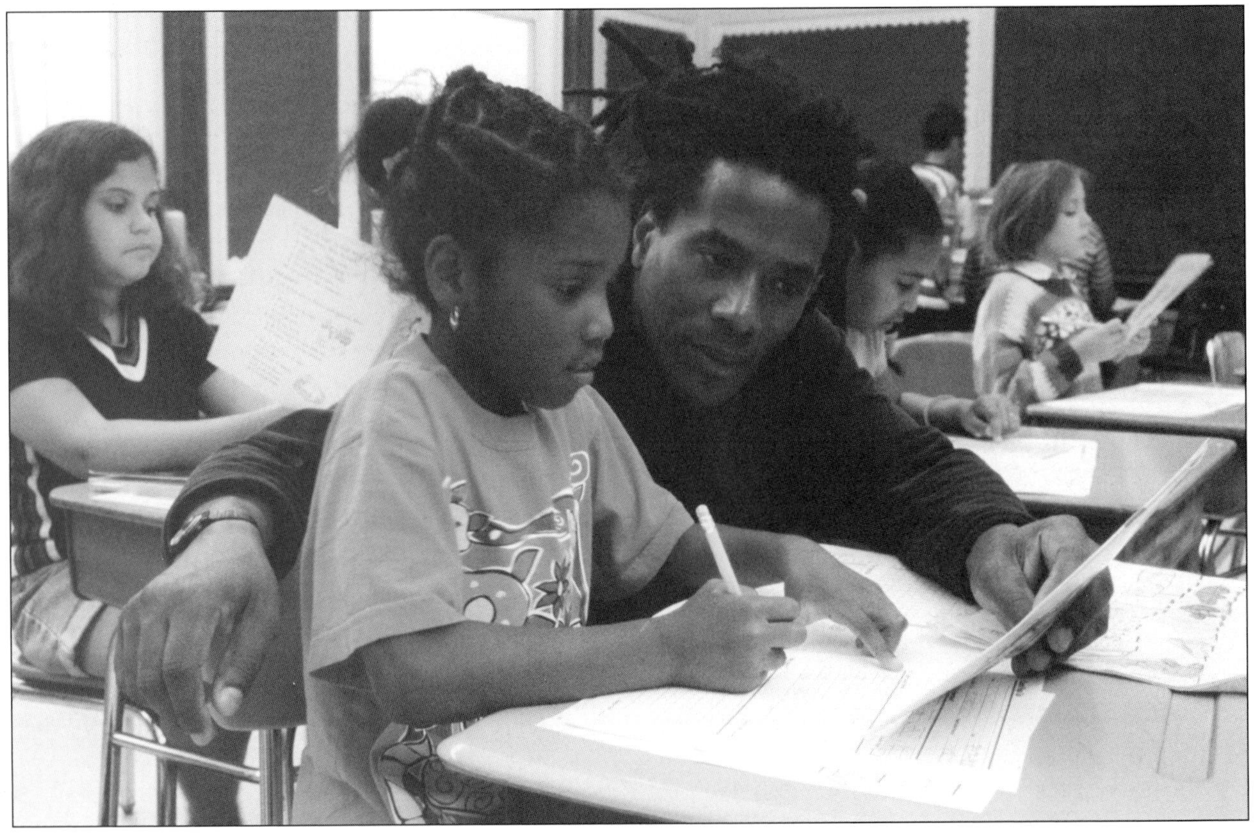

sun. Activity centers around the classroom are well organized, containing puppets, stuffed animals, props, paints, paper, and plenty of writing materials.

But what is most inspiring is watching Mr. Carter teach. For about two hours during reading period, he tirelessly keeps the children moving in an upbeat and energized pace from one interesting and valuable activity to the next.

When reading period begins, the children get their personal baskets of books and sit at their tables reading independently. Mr. Carter also has them read in pairs—shoulder to shoulder—or in small groups in circles on the floor. During this time, he takes the opportunity to move around the classroom and provide personalized attention. With one child, he reviews the previous day's word attack lesson. With a small group, he sits down on the floor and begins asking questions, helping them make meaningful connections between the literature and their own lives.

Now it is time for today's word attack lesson. The children put away their baskets and gather around Mr. Carter at the board. Each child sits on the floor holding a personal eraser board and magic marker. Clearly these new tools bring an aura of importance to the small hands holding them. Perhaps it is the authoritative thick marker, or the teacher-like power to erase. Perhaps it is the power of having one's very own tableau. Beyond being fun, the boards also give children privacy to make mistakes and easily correct themselves.

Mr. Carter begins by reading a sentence he has written on the board. Certain parts of the words are covered up. When he comes to the word "kind," he says it aloud, but what the children see is k___. He asks them to provide the missing letters. After various responses, correct and incorrect, he reveals the correctly spelled "kind." He then asks children to write the words "find" and "mind" on their boards. He proceeds doing a similar exercise with a number of words.

Now it is time for a class read-aloud time, in which children sit in a circle for two books, one fiction and the other nonfiction. Because it happens to be the end of the school year, both books are related to the theme of summer vacation.

The students are engaged and eager to participate. They sit in an orderly way, enthusiastically raising hands to answer questions instead of calling out. (This is protocol that Mr. Carter requires.) Mr. Carter pauses frequently, asking questions about the characters, plot, and meaning of the text. He also makes time for the children to ask some questions of their own.

At the beginning of the second hour, Mr. Carter gives a writing assignment. The children are to write a letter to a friend, describing their plans or hopes for summer vacation. When they are finished, they go to the computers to illustrate something from their writing. If time allows, they will then move on to their journals. Because the classroom has only six computers, he breaks the students into rotating groups.

Mr. Carter moves easily among groups, checking on his students' progress. Some children at the computer need encouragement. They don't know how to go about illustrating their writing. He talks through some options with them. When working with the children who are writing, he praises efforts to logically sound out new spellings—even if their final product is incorrect. But when he sees students misspell previously introduced words, such as "find" (taught that very day), he is sure to make a correction. Casually picking up a book or a word card, he says, "Remember the last time we saw this word in a book, it was spelled this way."

For a student who is having trouble with the writing assignment because she obviously didn't understand the story, Mr. Carter retrieves the book and asks an aide to read it again to the child. For another child, whose discomfort with the mechanics of holding a pen and writing gets in the way of even beginning to write, he assists by taking dictation. For children who have successfully completed the assignment before the others, Mr. Carter sets up groups of two, encouraging them to take turns reading to one another and polishing their newly finished creations.

published reading programs. One major benefit of these materials is that they provide a year-long plan for instruction—an essential element for effective teaching. However, even the most well-equipped children may not move with equal ease through any preset sequence of lessons. Teachers must adapt and augment their lessons to meet the unique needs of every one of the individual children in their classrooms. Most children need a motivating introduction and a lot of repetition and practice in order for their emerging skills to become automatic.

When children begin to read, they need the opportunity to read independently each day, choosing some texts themselves. These materials must be of high quality and of a difficulty level appropriate to the individual. Repeated readings of easy texts help children practice and assimilate what they've learned. Books that are more difficult give them a chance to move, and sometimes leap, ahead. Texts that appeal to their personal passions help them build a lifelong love of reading.

School leadership is responsible for making sure that reading instruction is coherent, that is, there is a consistent approach across the grades and that the teachers in the later grades know what the teachers before them have done.

We teach in small groups, whole group, and one on one—depending on the needs of the kids. We read literature to the whole class. Then, when we do reading instruction, we may put three children together who need the same thing. It's about finding out what children know and moving to the unknown.

Each child comes to school with a backpack. And in that backpack, each one has something different. Some have lots of experience with books and magnetic letters. Others have been living in an apartment with 15 people. What drives me to teach is watching what goes into those backpacks over the years.

—Emelie Parker
First grade teacher
Bailey's Elementary School
Fairfax County, Virginia

The Kindergarten Challenge

One major goal of kindergarten has always been to help children become comfortable in a formal classroom setting. Indeed, it is a major adjustment. Five-year-old children who enter kindergarten must learn how to sit quietly, to share, to listen, to communicate cooperatively, and to do what is asked. Even in the most individualized class, they must make do with far less personal attention than they probably are used to. Helping children meet this emotional and behavioral challenge is extremely important.

But kindergarten must also prepare children to learn to read, and this must be a key priority. Children enter kindergarten with different preschool reading and writing experiences: some write with scribbling and others with letters; some have lots of storybooks in their past and recite them eagerly; for others, books seem pretty unfamiliar. Research consistently demonstrates that children need to enter first grade with good attitudes and knowledge about literacy. Otherwise, they will probably find first grade instruction inaccessible.

What Must Be Accomplished—Goals of Kindergarten

The delicate balance for the kindergarten teacher is to promote literacy in well-thought-out, appropriate ways. Two goals are paramount:

- When children leave kindergarten, they should have a solid familiarity with the structure and uses of print. They should know about the format of books and other print resources. They should be familiar with sentence-by-sentence, word-by-word, and sound-by-sound analysis of language. They should achieve basic phonemic awareness and the ability to recognize and write most of the letters of the alphabet.
- Kindergarten should help children get comfortable with learning from print, since much of their future education will depend on this. By the end of the year, kindergartners should have an interest in the types of language and knowledge that books can bring them.

In this following section we present activities for kindergarteners. As for the earlier sets of activities, the main purpose is to illustrate the concepts underlying reading instruction in kindergarten. We expect that the individual activities included will be helpful for most children; however, they are not a substitute for a comprehensive curriculum.

Activities and Practices For Kindergartners

In kindergarten, it is especially appropriate for instruction to be based in play activities. By singing songs and acting out stories and situations, children develop language skills, narrative abilities, and a comfort with using symbols, that is, the idea that one thing can "stand for" something else. These are key for learning to read. We describe a range of activities that teachers can use in their classrooms. Many of them incorporate play-based instruction.

Book and Print Awareness

To become successful readers, children must understand how books and print work. They should know the parts of a book and their functions and that the print on the page represents the words that can be read aloud. By kindergarten, they can begin to distinguish various forms and purposes of print, from personal letters and signs to storybooks and essays.

Activities

Do dictation activities to help kindergartners understand that any thing spoken can be written. You can turn this into a major bookmaking project, collecting oral stories that children dictate, illustrate, and share with one another. And you can do frequent short dictations, writing down children's captions or titles for their artwork, or writing their shopping lists for pretend play. As part of these activities, help children notice various aspects of how print works: text is read from left to right and top to bottom; words are separated by spaces; the end of a line is not always the end of a thought.

Phonological Awareness

During the preschool years, most children spontaneously acquire some degree of ability to think about the sounds of spoken words, independent of their meanings: phonological awareness. In kindergarten, it is especially important to strengthen this initial insight, and especially to help children develop an awareness of the smallest meaningful units or phonemes that make up spoken words (a skill that is termed "phonemic awareness"). This is a crucial step toward understanding the alphabetic principle (that phonemes are what letters stand for) and, ultimately, toward learning to read.

Activities and Practices for Kindergartners

Activities

Many of the activities described earlier for use with preschoolers (pages 47 and48) are also appropriate for kindergartners.

Play the game SNAP using shared sounds. It's an excellent time passer during long car rides. One player says two words. If they share a sound, the other players say "snap" and snap their fingers. If the two words don't share a sound, everyone is quiet. Take turns. Begin with first sounds and go on to middle and final sounds when the child can do the first sound well. For example,

Player 1 says, "ball and bat."	The others say, "SNAP!" for the first sound.
Player 2 says, "sand and book."	Everyone is quiet.
Next player says, "run and tan."	The others say, "SNAP!" for the last sound.
Next player says, "seed and beach."	The others say, "SNAP!" for the middle sound.

Be prepared for things to get a little silly.

Tell children that you are going to play a listening game with them. Give out four blocks or some other tangible item, like card chips or beads, that can be used for counting phonemes. Remember to count sounds, not letters. These are spoken words, not written ones.

1. Say a two-phoneme word, such as "row," and ask the children to repeat it. Then say, "I can divide the word 'row' into two parts: 'r' and 'o'. Let's make this block stand for the 'o' part. We need both blocks together, 'r' and 'o,' to make 'row'." Have the children do this with their blocks. In this exercise, whenever you refer to a particular phoneme, touch the block that represents that segment.

   Next explain that a new word can be made by taking away the first block (the 'r' part). Have everyone take away the first block, and ask what the remaining block "says," namely the word "oh." Then ask what will happen if the first block is put back. Help the children to realize that the blocks now represent the word "row" again.

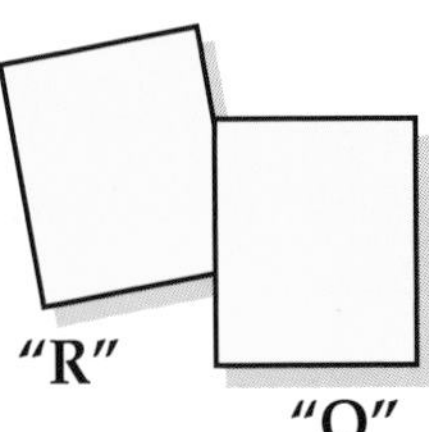

Next explain that another word can be made by adding a new block in front of the "r." This new block stands for "g," so when "g" and "r" and "o" are put together, we get the word "grow." Next, ask the children to add a block after the "o"; this new block stands for "n." Help them to understand that the four blocks now represent the four phonemes in "groan." Finally, have them remove the "n" block, leaving "grow" again.

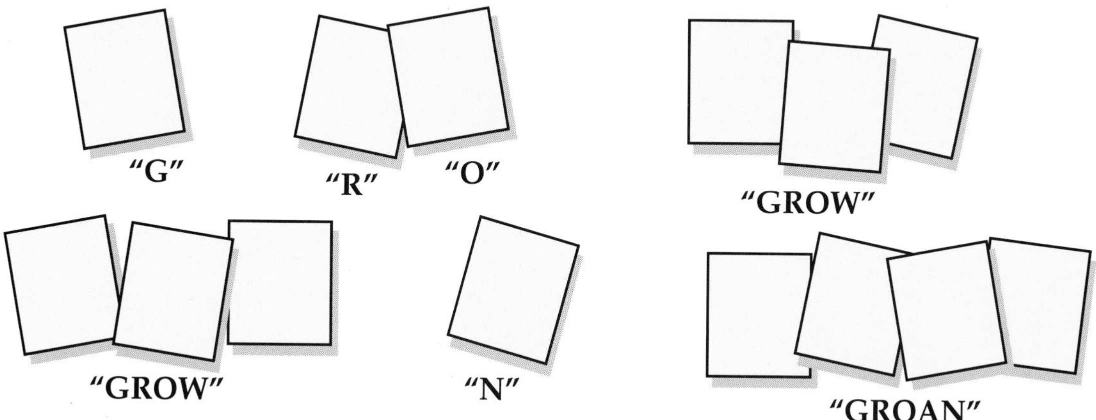

2. After this introduction, tell children that you now want three blocks to stand for a different word, "lamb." So now the first block is for the "l" part, the second block is for the "a" part, and the third block is for the "m" part. Now ask, "If I want to make the word "am," should I take away one of the blocks or should I add another block? (Answer: take away the first block.) And if I want to make the word "lamb" again, what must I do? (Answer: put it back.) And if I want to make the word "lamp," what should I do? (Answer: add a new block after the "m".)

   Repeat this exercise, sometimes first giving a word that requires removing a phoneme, and sometimes one that requires adding a new phoneme. Here are some words you can use:

Starting words	Words requiring removal	Words requiring addition
late	ate	plate
gray	ray	great
pin	in	spin (or pinch)
tore	or	store
rice	ice	price
care	air	scare
rain	ray	train
bad	add	band
goat	go	ghost
mall	all	small

Do a listening game in which you have children blend your pronunciation of onset (the first part of a syllable) and rime (the ending part) into a meaningful one syllable target word.

- Tell children that you are going to say a word broken into parts and that you need them to put the word back together. Begin by saying simple words aloud, pausing between the onset and the rime. At first, vary the onset and keep the same rime:

  r . . . an
  m . . . an
  f . . . an

  Then keep the onset and vary the rime. For example,

  m . . . an
  m . . . ice
  m . . . ix

- Expand the activity by saying a word and asking children to provide another that ends with the same sound—i.e., rhymes.

Language, Comprehension, and Response to Text

Texts can give us great ideas, entertaining stories, knowledge, information, and countless other riches. But children who lack vocabulary and a useful repertoire of general knowledge can barely take the first step toward the most basic understanding of the texts they encounter. How can they understand a science book about volcanoes, a fairy tale about silkworms, or a short story about Inuits if they don't understand the words "volcanoes," "silkworms," or "Inuits"? What if they know nothing of mountains, caterpillars, or snow and cold climates? Kindergartners need the chance to build their general background knowledge and language if they are to understand and profit from the texts they will encounter.

Another important factor in understanding text is interest. Children need to be interested in books and print, if they are going to read enough to get good at it. One important goal of kindergarten is to motivate children to relate to books and print as a meaningful and worthwhile part of their lives.

Rich classroom discussions, thoughtful question-and-answer periods, fun, engaging activities connected to texts, high-quality storybook readings—all these have an important place in helping children move, day by day, toward understanding what they read, enjoying it, and becoming real readers. i

New Words, New Ideas

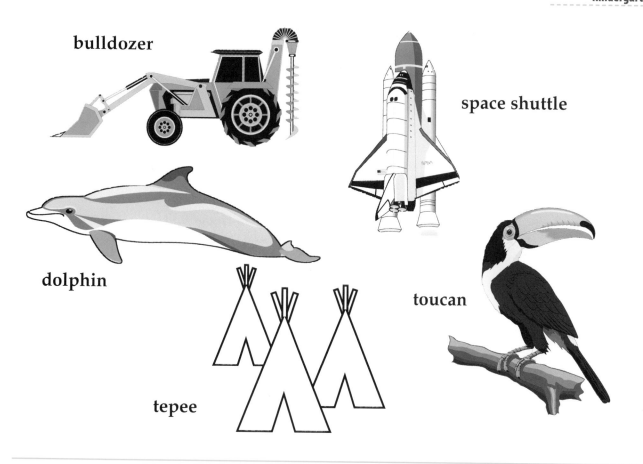

Activities and Practices for **Kindergartners**

bulldozer

space shuttle

dolphin

toucan

tepee

Activities

Help children develop the knowledge and vocabulary they will need to become successful readers.

- Take children on excursions and field trips to interesting places that will give them new domains of knowledge and vocabulary. For example, a class visit to a farm can be introduced and followed with rich class discussion about food and farming, in which you and the children use new words and concepts, such as "tractor," "milking," "plow," "fields," "planting." Also, elicit individual conversations in which children have a chance to describe what they have seen.

Activities and Practices for **Kindergartners**

- Set up a sharing time when children can bring in objects or concepts of interest to them for discussion. Create an enriching conversational environment by responding to the sharer and expanding on his or her thoughts, inviting other children to participate.

Use the above opportunities to inspire classroom discussions—both in a one-to-one and a whole-class format. Affirm children in their efforts to express themselves, but also gently nudge them to be more precise in their vocabulary and syntax. Enhance their syntactic abilities beyond the usual "and then, and then, and then," by asking questions that encourage them to use words like "because," "after," "since," and "while" in their responses. If a child says, "I ate a red lollipop," you might help him or her be more precise by saying, "But there could be two different red lollipops. Did you have strawberry or cherry?"

Choose books and stories to read aloud that are about many different creatures, places, and things. Augment each selection with pictures, discussion, and especially other books and stories that allow the children to revisit and extend their new knowledge.

Sociodramatic play activities give children a chance to develop language and literacy skills, a deeper understanding of narrative, and their own personal responses to stories. Encourage children to retell, reenact, or dramatize stories or parts of stories they have read.

The possibilities for sociodramatic play are limitless and need not be related only to fiction. For example, one class decided to embark on a dinosaur dig after reading about dinosaurs. They cordoned off a small grassy area outside the school and began digging. One after another, children would finds sticks and stones that they would proclaim to be remnants of dinosaurs, such as triceratops or tyrannosaurus. The teacher helped them incorporate literacy by making signs for the digging area ("Dinosaur Dig—Do Not Disturb") and by labeling the children's findings. The endeavor led to further book reading about dinosaurs, discussions about science, and rich conversations.

Here are some tips for successful sociodramatic play:

- Prepare the environment. Make sure children have the necessary materials, such as puppets, stuffed animals, building blocks, props, and writing materials (so they can use print in their play). The best classrooms usually offer thematic centers that appeal to student interests—such as a nature area, a puppet theater, a sand table decked out as a beach—along with books, stories, and trips related to the theme.

- Provide ample time for children to create scripts and scenarios. Develop their background knowledge for the play setting

- Encourage and guide rehearsals of dramatic retellings. Take part in the action yourself, demonstrating for children ways in which dramatization works.

- Guide children in dramatizations that involve print—for example, a restaurant scene that requires a menu and a pad to write down food orders—reinforced by explanations of how menus work.

Activities and Practices for Kindergartners

Help children develop listening skills by offering books on tape and by playing games in which you call out oral directions and instructions for them to follow. You might also try call-and-response songs, such as the classic recording "Follow the Leader" by Ella Jenkins, in which children are asked to clap and beat out rhythms to music in various ways.

Good storybook reading is an interactive process that helps children explore language and develop many skills. Offer a variety of texts, nonfiction as well as fiction. Here are some effective techniques for reading aloud:

- Have children ask their own questions about the story and respond to classmates' questions.
- Encourage them to follow the text with movement, mime, or choral reading.
- Draw children's attention to the forms of print, such as punctuation, letters, the space around words, chapter title placement, the line length differences between prose and poetry.
- Provide repeated readings of the same story so children can gain mastery of the narrative, ideas, and language.
- When reading chapter books to children, ask them to summarize before and after you read each chapter. "So where are we so far?" you might ask at the beginning of the session. And then at the end, "So what happened in this chapter?"

Pair or group children together for shared book experiences. Or put children who have the same interests together and start book clubs in your class. In the book club format, help them read the same or similar books and discuss them with one another. Teachers might use parent volunteers to come in and help with reading or discussions in the clubs. Or children can bring home books to be read with parents and report on them the next day in their book clubs.

Give children access to a wide variety of reading materials.

Connecting to Books

It is the day before Thanksgiving break, and the kindergartners gather in a circle for story time. Whereas a few months ago, the children in her class had trouble sitting still, now they listen attentively, ready to answer Mrs. Harris's questions.

Today's book is about a child whose grandmother has come from another country to visit for Thanksgiving. Much is made of the enormous hug that she gives her grandchild at the airport.

Mrs. Harris pauses from the story. "Does anyone have relatives who like to give hugs when they come an visit?" Her purpose is to help children learn to connect information and events in texts to real life.

Half a dozen hands shoot up eagerly. One by one, she hears accounts of hugging relatives—Mae, whose grandmother squeezed her tight when she went to Vietnam; Andre, whose aunt hugged him when she came from Guiana; Molly, whose grandfather hugged her when he came from Minnesota. After each child speaks, Mrs. Harris repeats the response, often asking the child to elaborate in some way, or add more detail.

Finally, after listening to six or seven accounts, Mrs. Harris remarks, "Isn't it interesting that so many families from so many different places all like to hug their kids. You seem to have something in common with the child in this story. Okay, let's go back and read the rest," she says and resumes reading. The children are quiet again, hanging on to her every word.

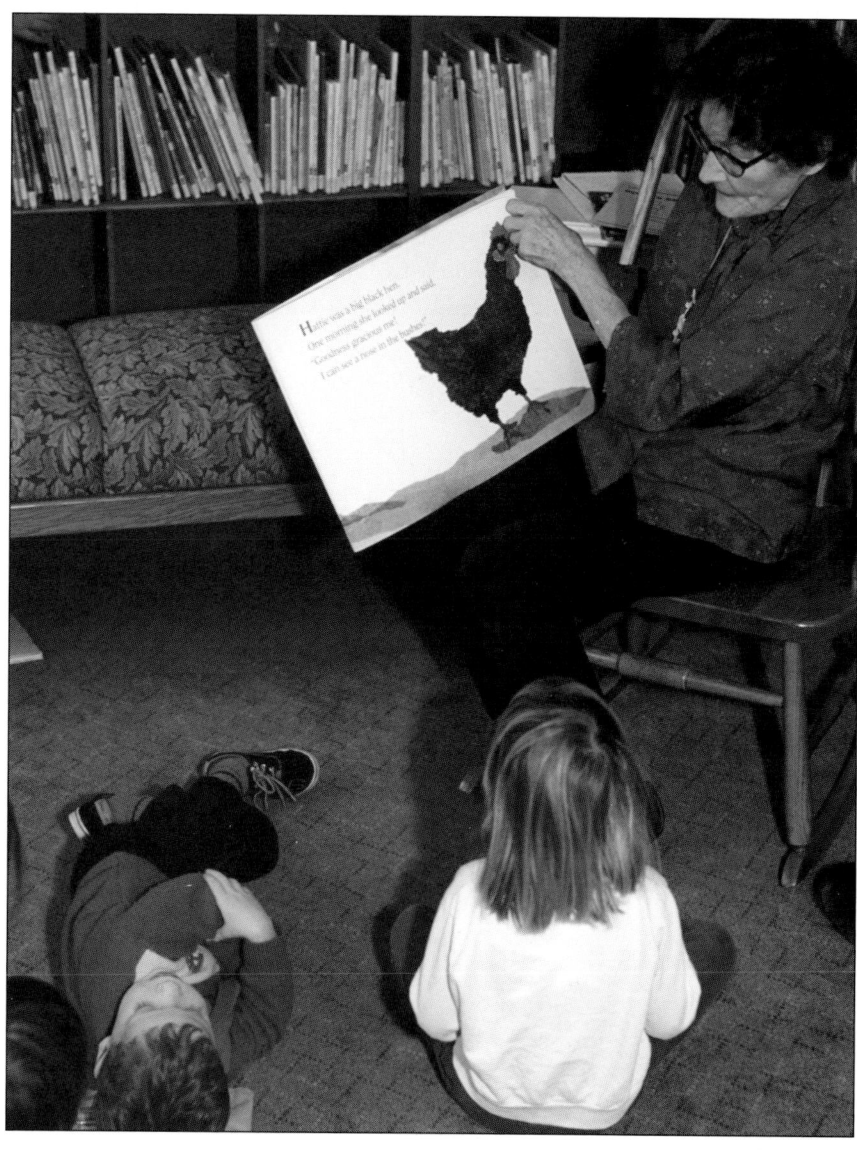

- Give children guidance and suggestions for choosing appropriate reading materials that appeal to their interests and reading ability. Give them a chance to choose their own books in their class library, their school library, and their local public library. Help them to develop familiarity with a number of books and authors. For example, if they like a certain book, suggest that they look for another by the same author, or on a similar theme.

- Help children develop familiarity with a number of types or genres of texts. Stock your class library center with a variety of materials, including storybooks, nonfiction, poems, newspapers, and magazines.

- Other activity centers can include print from everyday life, such as take-out menus, this week's cafeteria menu, seasonal toy catalogs, and class rosters that are kept current.

"At the beginning of the school year, one of the first things I do is send applications for library cards home with my students. Each child is issued a card, and I take the children to the library. I give parents a list of approved books. Many parents tell me they don't know how to read well. If they can't read to the child, I tell them to find someone who can."

—Ethelyn Hamilton-Frezel
Kindergarten teacher
Dr. Ronald E. McNair Elementary School
New Orleans, Louisiana

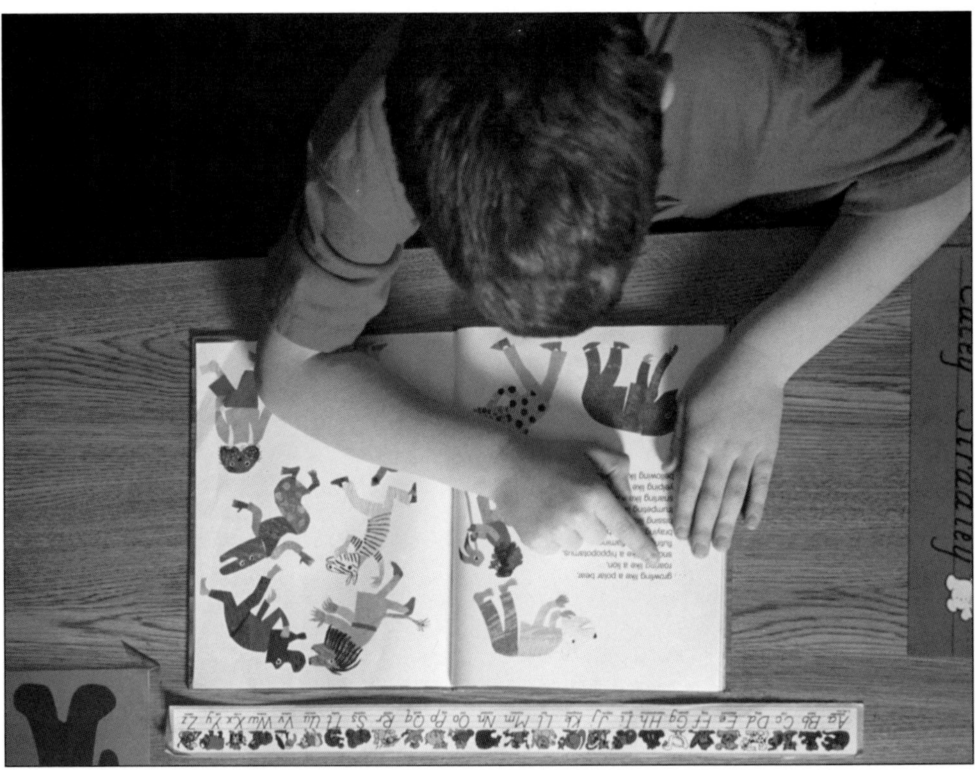

Letter Recognition, Decoding, and Word Recognition

By the end of kindergarten, children should be able to name most of the letters of the alphabet, no matter what order they come in, no matter if they are in uppercase or lowercase. And they should do it quickly and effortlessly. They should begin to learn about letter-sound correspondence and to decode simple words. They should begin to recognize some very common words by sight.

Activities

Establish a routine so that each child in the class has a day that is his or her Letter Day. On a given child's day, put up his or her initials on a part of the bulletin or chalk board. For example, on Aaron Smith's day, the teacher puts up the letters "A" and "S." All day long, the children are to be on alert for words in their environment containing "A's" or "S's." When they find one, they should whisper it to an adult. The adult will then make an announcement at the appropriate moment, saying something like "Jessica sees a letter 'A' in the science area. The word she sees is 'ants'." The teacher can then point to the poster of ants, then write the word on the chalk board.

Bb
G I R A F F E R A J J C
E A G L E K J H L H U R
I B E X A T D I L E N O
J L J N L I O N I R G C
Z A S W J G L O G O J O
P E O E L E P H A N T D
U S B E A R H T T J J I
M J A R J J I W O L F L
A J T J A E N A R C J E
Big Dog
BRICKS
Big Dog Gets in Trouble
Book

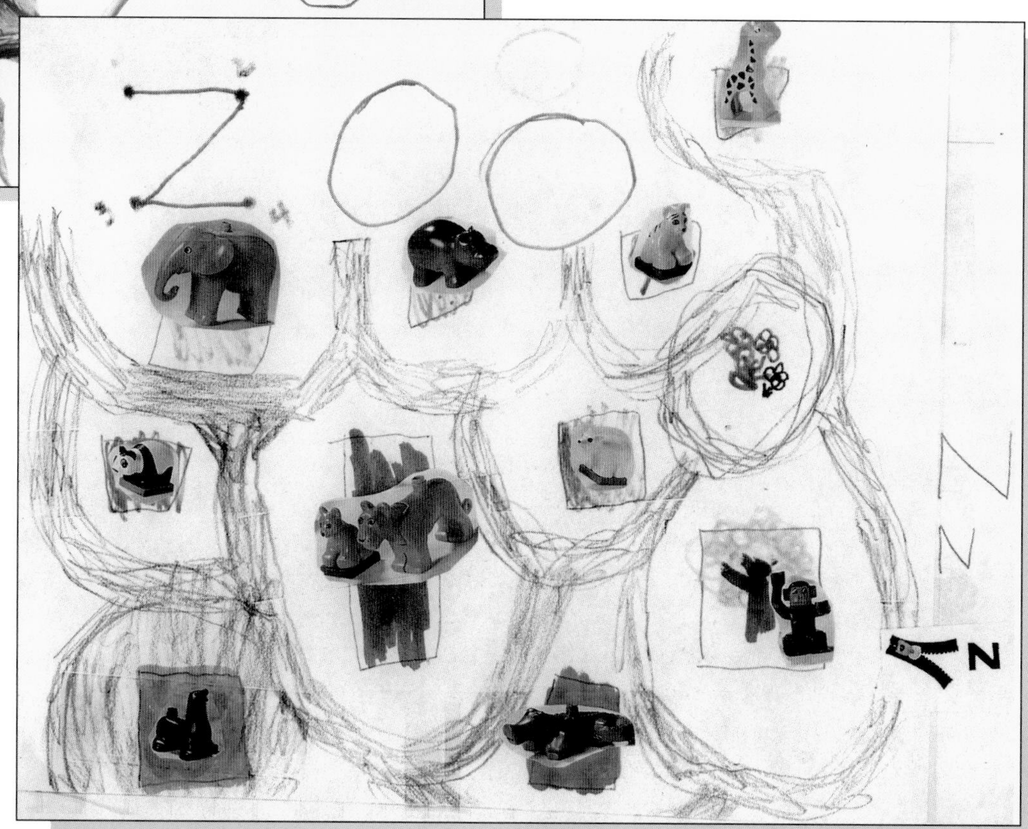
ZOO
N

Help children get increasingly comfortable with recognizing and naming all uppercase and lowercase letters of the alphabet. One fun way to do this is to play an adaptation of the old favorite game, I Spy. Reuse some piece of text that all children can have in front of them, for example, a photocopied paragraph in a book that matches one of the teacher's big books. Ask all children to focus on the text. Start the game by saying, "I spy with my little eye, seven small letter 't's'." In this way, challenge children to locate all the small letter 't's' in the passage. (Remember, they are not supposed to be reading the text, just looking for the letter and getting comfortable with recognizing it in uppercase and lowercase forms.) Allow children to take turns being the spy.

Show children that the sequence of letters in a written word matches the sequence of sounds they hear when the word is spoken.

- On the board, write a simple word that begins with a consonant. Direct the children to sound, blend, and identify the word. Swap the initial consonant with another consonant and ask them to say the new word. Demonstrate the sounding and blending of the letters for them. Repeat this exercise often. After children have mastered swapping the initial consonant, try replacing the final consonants. On any given day, however, it is best to focus on one letter position at a time. After children have had some experience, try the harder task of switching the vowel sounds.

Initial consonant swap:	bat, cat, hat, mat, pat, sat, vat
Final consonant swap:	fit, fin, fib, fig
Vowel sound:	pat, pet, pit, pot *or* bit, bat, bet, but

Tip: Don't forget Dr. Seuss books, such as *Green Eggs and Ham* and *One Fish Two Fish*, which offer lively and fun prose filled with rhymes and word play that you can integrate into your lessons.

Help children build their sight vocabulary. Try this word card game, a version of the parlor game Concentration. Make or gather two copies of 6 word cards, for a total of 12 cards (2 cards for each of 6 words). Shuffle the cards and lay them out in rows of three by four, face down. The first player turns over two cards and read each word that is turned over. If two cards match, the player takes the cards and gets another turn. If they don't match, the player must put them back exactly in the same place, face down. Then the next player tries. Using his or her memory about the cards previously revealed, he or she gets to turn over another two cards, trying to get a match. Play until all cards have been matched. Read all the words after the game. Play more than once to practice words. Add new words. Words like the following are good to start with, because they will be encountered frequently in books and are somewhat irregular in their spelling:

the
one
two
says
said
have

Writing Time

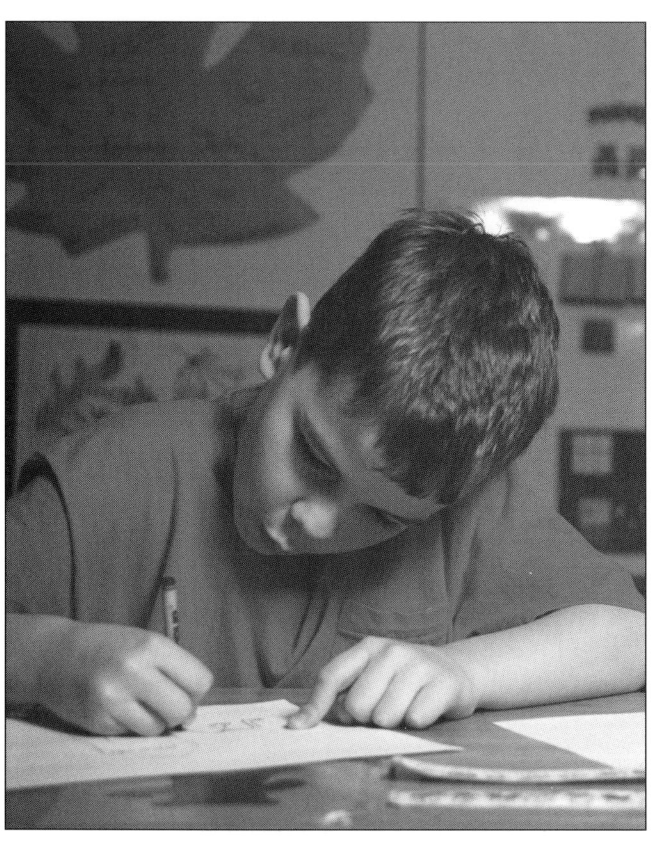

It is writing time, and the kindergartners are sitting in chairs with paper and pencil before them. Their assignment: to write about the weather that day. Mrs. Miller is moving about the classroom, coaching individual children in this endeavor.

"Read to me, Amir."

Amir is now looking out of the window at the clouds. He picks up his writing and reads, "Today is cloudy. I hope it will snow." On his paper is printed:

Toda iz clody I hop it wil sno

"Good," says Mrs. Miller. She points to the word "toda," and says. "I can figure this word out; this one is almost like how I spell it. She points to the word "Today" on the blackboard.

"What would you do if it snows?" she asks.

"Make a snowman," replies Amir instantly.

"Why don't you write that down and some other things you like to do in the snow. Then draw a picture to go with it. Make sure you put yourself in the story and in the picture. I want to see you in the snow."

Intrigued, Amir leans over his paper and continues working.

Activities and Practices for **Kindergartners**

Help children learn to recognize common but irregularly spelled words such as "the," "have," and "two." One excellent way is through familiar nursery rhymes. For example, write on the board and recite:

Hickory dickory dock.
The mouse went up the clock.
The clock struck one. The mouse ran down.
Hickory dickory dock.

Have children join in on the rhyme, and point to each word as it is read. Then write the word "the" and "The" on the board. Point to one line at a time and call on children to come to the board to touch the word "the" if it appears. Tell them that the word "the" is a word they see a lot when they read. Put the word on the wall with other words like "the" that will occur freqently in text. These words should be taught as sight words so they are recognized instantly.

Spelling and Writing

Children need ample opportunity to write. Stock the kindergarten classroom with a variety of paper, writing utensils, and materials for book-making (glue, tape, stapler, book covers). Early in the kindergarten year, some children may still be scribbling and drawing pictures. By the end of the year, they will be independently writing most uppercase and lowercase letters, using invented spellings for many words, and working on a growing repertoire of conventionally spelled words.

Activities

Have children make their own letter dictionaries. Each child will need his or her own notebook, pencils, pens, crayons, markers, old magazines, safety scissors, and paste or tape. This is a year-long project.

- Gather each child's notebook and print each letter of the alphabet on the head of a single page—skipping some pages between each letter. Remember to print both uppercase and lowercase letters. When you are ready to proceed, pass out the books to the children, telling them that these books are going to become their personal letter dictionaries.

Elisa
My
Dictionary

- Have the children find conventionally spelled words to copy on the appropriate page. Encourage them to draw a picture of the thing, if possible, or to paste in a picture from an old magazine.

- Use the dictionaries as a way to reinforce class activities and lessons with letters and words. For example, when it is Zakary Feinstein's letter day, you might write some "z" or "f" words on the board and ask the children to copy them on the appropriate page in their dictionary.

Accomplishments of the Kindergarten Student

Kindergarten is a great time of preparation for the challenge of real reading. Toward this end, we list a particular set of accomplishments that the successful learner should exhibit by the end of kindergarten. Because of their importance, we present them in full, as published in *Preventing Reading Difficulties in Young Children* (National Academy Press, 1998). As with the list of accomplishments for the preschool child, this list is neither exhaustive nor incontestable, but it does capture many highlights of the course of literacy acquisition. Although the timing of these accomplishments will vary among children, they are the sorts of things that should be in place when children enter first grade.

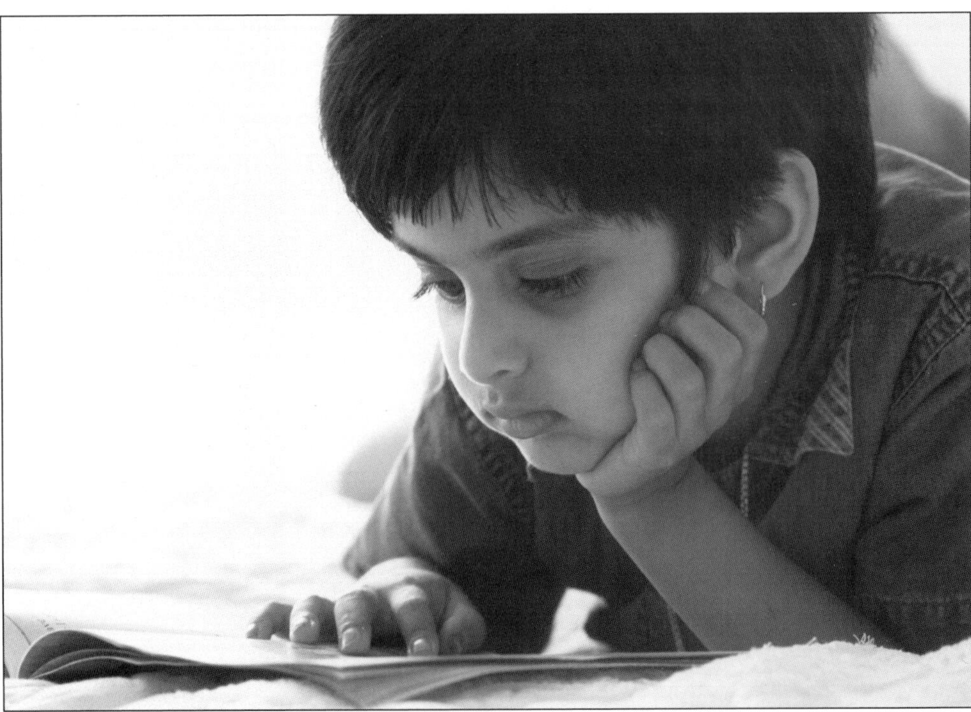

Kindergarten Accomplishments

- Knows the parts of a book and their functions.
- Begins to track print when listening to a familiar text being read or when rereading own writing.
- "Reads" familiar texts emergently, i.e., not necessarily verbatim from the print alone.
- Recognizes and can name all uppercase and lowercase letters.
- Understands that the sequence of letters in a written word represents the sequence of sounds (phonemes) in a spoken word (alphabetic principle).
- Learns many, though not all, one-to-one letter-sound correspondences.
- Recognizes some words by sight, including a few very common ones ("the," "I," "my," "you," "is," "are").
- Uses new vocabulary and grammatical constructions in own speech.
- Makes appropriate switches from oral to written language styles.
- Notices when simple sentences fail to make sense.
- Connects information and events in texts to life and life experiences to text.
- Retells, reenacts, or dramatizes stories or parts of stories.
- Listens attentively to books the teacher reads to class.
- Can name some book titles and authors.
- Demonstrates familiarity with a number of types or genres of text (e.g., storybooks, expository texts, poems, newspapers, and everyday print such as signs, notices, labels).
- Correctly answers questions about stories read aloud.
- Makes predictions based on illustrations or portions of stories.
- Demonstrates understanding that spoken words consist of sequences of phonemes.
- Given spoken sets like "dan, dan, den," can identify the first two as the same and the third as different.
- Given spoken sets like "dak, pat, zen," can identify the first two as sharing one same sound.
- Given spoken segments, can merge them into a meaningful target word.
- Given a spoken word, can produce another word that rhymes with it.
- Independently writes many uppercase and lowercase letters.
- Uses phonemic awareness and letter knowledge to spell independently (invented or creative spelling).
- Writes (unconventionally) to express own meaning.
- Builds a repertoire of some conventionally spelled words.
- Shows awareness of distinction between "kid writing" and conventional orthography.
- Writes own name (first and last) and the first names of some friends or classmates.
- Can write most letters and some words when they are dictated.

First Grade: An Important Year

"I don't think there is one best method of teaching reading or one best program. What I have done over my 27 years is pick what I think works and incorporate it. Every day, the children need to hear reading, and they need to be involved in the reading process. I do a lot of phonemic awareness with songs and games, as well as exposing them to a lot of print with labeling in the room. I do believe phonics is important. We also have a daily chit chat in which we talk to one another through writing. They write to me about their pets, their families, what they saw on television. Then the next day, I give them back a written response. It becomes an ongoing correspondence."

—Susan Derber
First grade teacher
Sandburg School
Springfield, Illinois

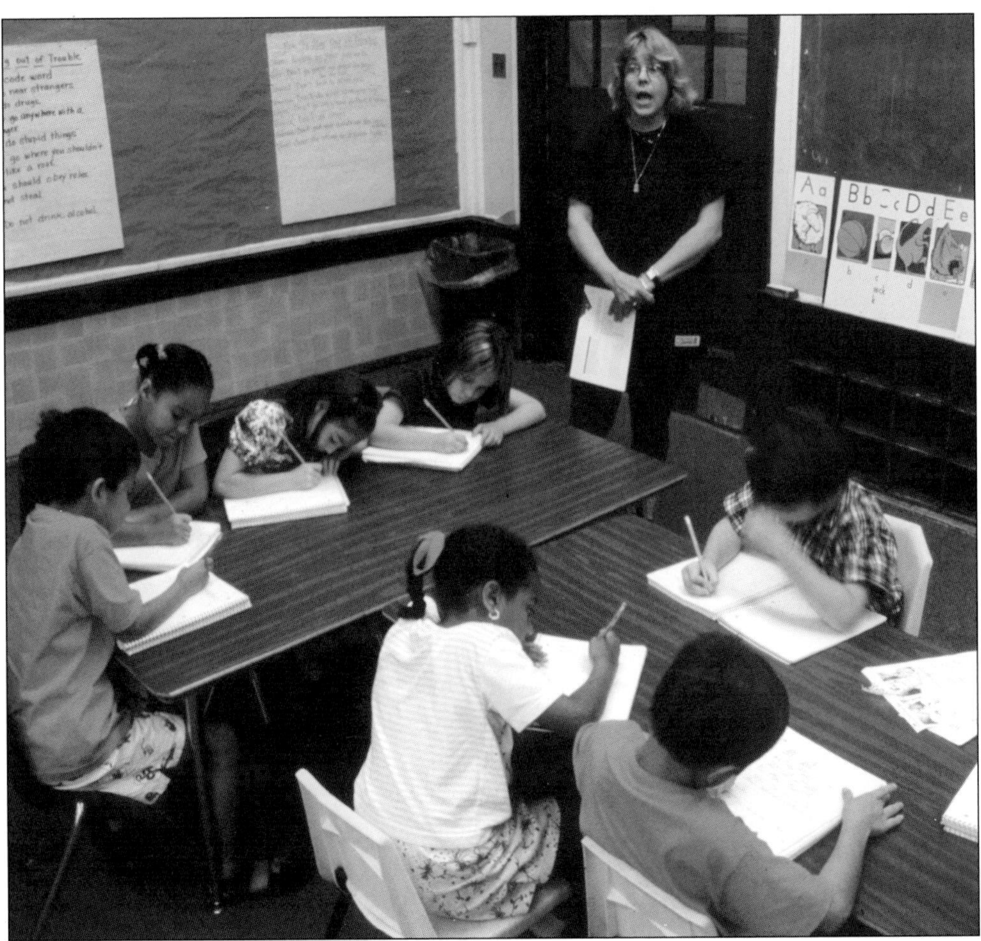

Although becoming literate is a lengthy process that begins in babyhood, first grade is a most important year. First graders enter school expecting to learn how to read on their own. Their parents and teachers expect this as well.

Anyone who has witnessed good teaching can attest that it is nothing short of an art, requiring remarkable talent, skill, and devotion. Teaching this age group, in particular, presents major challenges. In just about every school in America, some kids enter the first grade reading on a third grade level, whereas others are not able to reliably recognize all the letters of the alphabet. Teachers, most of them faced with more than 20 children, have to find ways to make sure that each child makes progress each day.

How do successful teachers accommodate the individual learning of so many very different first graders?

Sometimes they team with each other, even across grade levels, for small-group instruction suited to the abilities and interests of their students. Sometimes they set up groups within a class: the children benefit from working together, and the teacher is able to move around, focusing on a single group or taking time for one-on-one instruction with a struggling child. Sometimes teachers bring in volunteers or specialists to help challenge more advanced students or give individual help. Or they use whole-class activities designed to be interesting and successful even in classes with the most diverse mix of abilities.

All of these approaches—and many others—can work, so long as teachers avoid turning groupings into self-fulfilling prophecies that limit children. Always, teachers must sensitively monitor students' needs and progress to keep up the challenge and feed their students' curiosity, while avoiding frustrations and labels that can cause them to give up on themselves.

First grade is the time when children bring together the many language and literacy skills they have been attaining—book and print awareness, phonemic awareness, letter and word knowledge, background information about different topics—and start getting comfortable and quick with the conventions of associating letters and sounds. Ultimately, teachers must ensure that each child will not only read well, but also will enjoy reading and rely on it to learn new things as they move on with their lives. This is the year most children become "real" conventional readers, and most children depend strongly—some entirely—on teachers to guide this transition.

As in the previous section on kindergarten, in the following section we present activities for first graders in order to illustrate for family and community members, concepts underlying reading instruction. Many of the activities presented are ones expected to take place in the first half of the year. We expect that the individual activities included will be helpful for most children; however, they are examples rather than comprehensive curricula in themselves.

Features of Success

From parents to policy makers, an urgent question is: What does a good reading program look like?

There is no single answer, as each day, millions of children all over the country successfully learn to read under a great variety of approaches. What we do know, however, is that the most effective reading programs share certain common features, and that there are certain activities that all first grade children should be doing.

For a child to read fluently, he or she must recognize words at a glance, and use the conventions of letter-sound correspondences automatically. Without these word recognition skills, children will never be able to read or understand text comfortably and competently. Teachers help children with this hurdle by providing intense and intentional instruction on the structure of oral language and on the connections between phonemes and spellings.

In addition, first graders need intensive opportunities to read, each and every day, meaningful and engaging texts, both aloud with others and independently. In first grade and throughout the early grades, teachers should include explicit instruction on comprehension strategies, such as summarizing the main idea, predicting, and drawing inferences. In addition, first graders must have ample encouragement to write, even when this means using creative or inventive spelling.

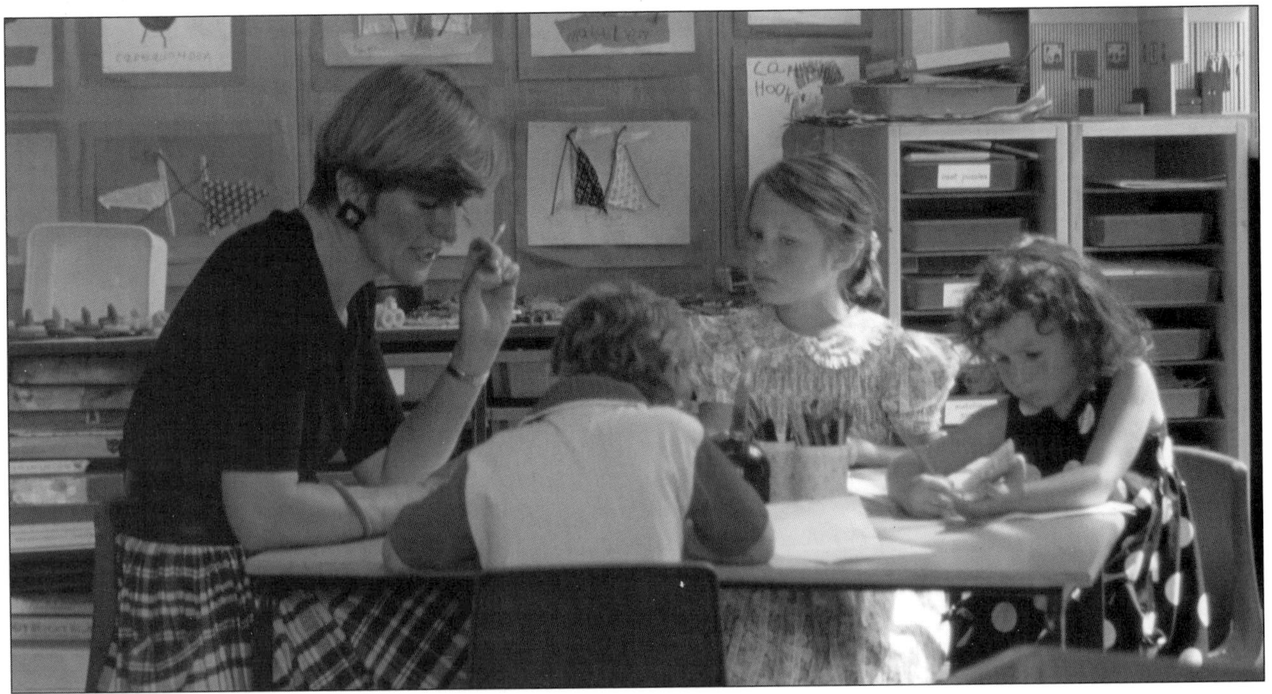

First Attempts

There's a birthday in the family today. Larry's little brother Evan has turned four. In the usual family tradition, everyone has gathered in the kitchen for a pancake breakfast. After the dishes are cleared, Evan is ready for birthday presents.

"Happy birthday, Evan," says Evan's father, putting down two wrapped boxes before him. Evan makes a grab for his presents—ready to tear at the wrapping paper. "Hey, Evan—what about the card?" asks his mother. Evan tears open the envelope. After a struggle, he pulls out a birthday card.

"Hey, it's a picture of a train!" he calls out. "I like trains." Then he points to a few letters he knows. "There's a 'B.' There's an 'O'." Then, while looking at the words on the inside of the card, he rapidly sings the Happy Birthday song to himself.

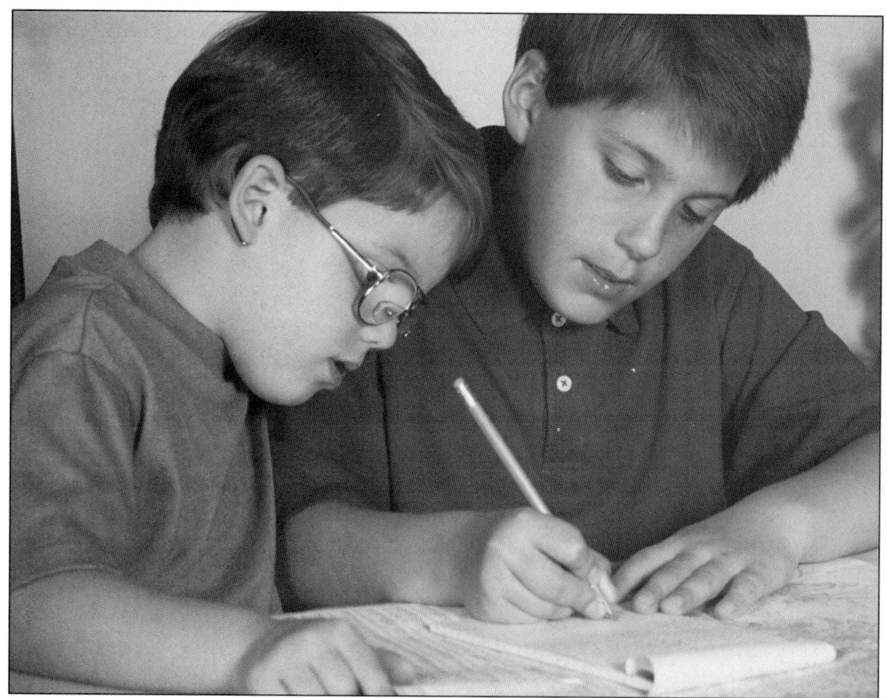

"Want me to really read the card?" asks his six-year-old brother. "I can read that card to you," says Larry, who takes the card and unceremoniously begins to read in a slow, halting tone, sounding out almost every word, getting help from Mom with some words.

"Ha ...ppy B..irth. . . day and m..a..ny more. Can h...ard..ly believe ...you are four!"

"Why, Larry!" reply both his parents simultaneously—they had never seen Larry do anything like this before. They eye one another with shock. This is the first time that Larry has ever volunteered to read something. In the past, they'd wondered if he was really reading books or reciting them. But he has never seen this card before, and so now they are sure: he has become a real reader.

Evan sets about tearing open his presents. One of his new treasures is a train set, the other is a book.

Evan turns to his brother and says, "Hey, Larry—will you read my new book to me?"

Finally, to help children understand the books they will encounter, reading classes—and all curricula in the primary grades—should help build their background knowledge and vocabulary in a rich variety of domains—from animals and the solar system to the ordinary workings of life, such as supermarkets and subways.

ACTIVITIES AND PRACTICES FOR FIRST GRADE CLASSROOMS

Continuing Phonemic Awareness, Letter Knowledge, and Book and Print Awareness

By first grade, many children have acquired some experience with phonemes in spoken language and with written letters, and they have a growing understanding about the uses and purposes of books and print. For children who need additional practice in these areas, some of the activities described in earlier sections of this book can be adapted with special content for first graders. Note that many of the following activities can be woven casually into daily first grade life, as children and teachers get to know each other. i

Activities

In this activity, you will have the children "break apart" and "put together" the syllables of words.

- Tell children you are going to play the Name Game. Go around the class, saying children's names, clapping and pausing with the syllables. For example, say "Sophia." Then say it with pauses between the syllables, "So. . . phi. . . a," while clapping once for each syllable. Do it again and ask children to join in. Go around the classroom, clapping out the syllables to various children's names. Count the number of claps and point out that some names get just one clap, and other names have many. Do a few children's names each day, during whole-class time.

- Just as important, make sure that children also can put words back together from their syllable parts. For example, say "So. . . phi. . . a," and ask the children to put the name back together. They should say, "Sophia."

When the children are confident and competent about the syllable-level activities, do similar activities working with phonemes, the smallest units of speech. Have children break apart and put together the separate phonemes of simple one-syllable words.

- Try connecting this activity to the personality of classmates. For example, use picture cards that represent simple one-syllable words and have each child pick a favorite card. Now, call on a child to hold the picture card up while you say the word. Then say it again, but this time with pauses and claps between each phoneme. For example, Sophia has a picture of a star. You say, "star," then you say each phoneme, "s. . . t. . . a. . . r," with a pause and clap for each. Let the class repeat it after you, or let Sophia pick other children to break the word apart.

The Beauty of the Alphabet

"It's not just drill and practice so kids can learn how to read good stories," says Ms. Jones, a first grade teacher for more than 10 years. "Sure, I love reading with children—it means the world to me. But the alphabetic principle is wonderful thing too, in and of itself."

She is talking to a young woman, a student teacher who appears about 20 years old. This is her first week on the job. Fresh from college, she has a passion for children's literature, and a respect for the necessity of spelling and phonics lessons—but hardly a love of it. One suspects she sees the alphabetic principle as a sort of medicine that has to be swallowed, rather than something that could be celebrated and loved.

"Imagine," says Ms. Jones. "First, you're just a young child and all the language you hear is a mysterious swirl of sound, and the words in your picture book are just little black marks. But then one day, you notice that there are some small sounds—phonemes—that you hear over and over again in different ways in different words around you. Take for example the "m" sound. It keeps coming up. You hear it in 'mommy'...'mailman'...'milk.'"

"Then you start to realize that you can manipulate phonemes yourself to make up all kinds of words. You can switch 'bat' into 'cat' and 'cake' into 'bake.' Now you've got phonemic awareness."

"Then you learn the letters of the alphabet. You've got these 26 lovely figures to record all these small sounds. Now you've got spelling or orthography. Even more thrilling: you can use those letters to recover the sounds that someone else recorded for your reading. Now you've got decoding and phonics."

"What an amazing system our alphabet is—and no one even really knows who invented it! But with the alphabet, everyone can read what anyone else has written, even people who do not know each other."

"That's some way to look at it," replies the student, clearly dazzled.

"You're darn right it is," says the teacher. "This is the gift I give children—the alphabetic principle. And that's why I love being a first grade teacher."

Ms. Jones walks off to her next class, leaving the student teacher standing amazed and a bit wide-eyed, listening anew to the sounds of children's language echoing through the hallways around her.

- On another day you and the child might keep the picture concealed at first. Together, say the phonemes, "s. . . t. . . a. . . r," with pauses between them. Ask the classmates to put the word together, rewarding them by showing the picture. Eventually, work on elaborations by getting the children to identify their mystery word in a sentence. For example, say "I looked up and saw the first s. . . t. . . a. . . r of the evening," and Sophia should answer by saying "star," and showing her picture.

As an elaboration of the letter dictionaries described in the kindergarten section, have each child make a personal alphabet file with 26 folders—one for each letter of the alphabet. They can make the files with folded construction paper. Have them write the letters, both upper- and lowercase, on index cards in each file. (The files can be kept in a box in the child's desk or cubby.) Over time, have them put names, other words, and pictures into the appropriate letter file. When new words come up in vocabulary lessons, reading, or other activities, ask the children to add them to their files. (An alternative to this is the use of an index card box. Each child has an index card box with dividers for each letter of the alphabet. Children put words, names, pictures on cards and file them under the appropriate letter.)

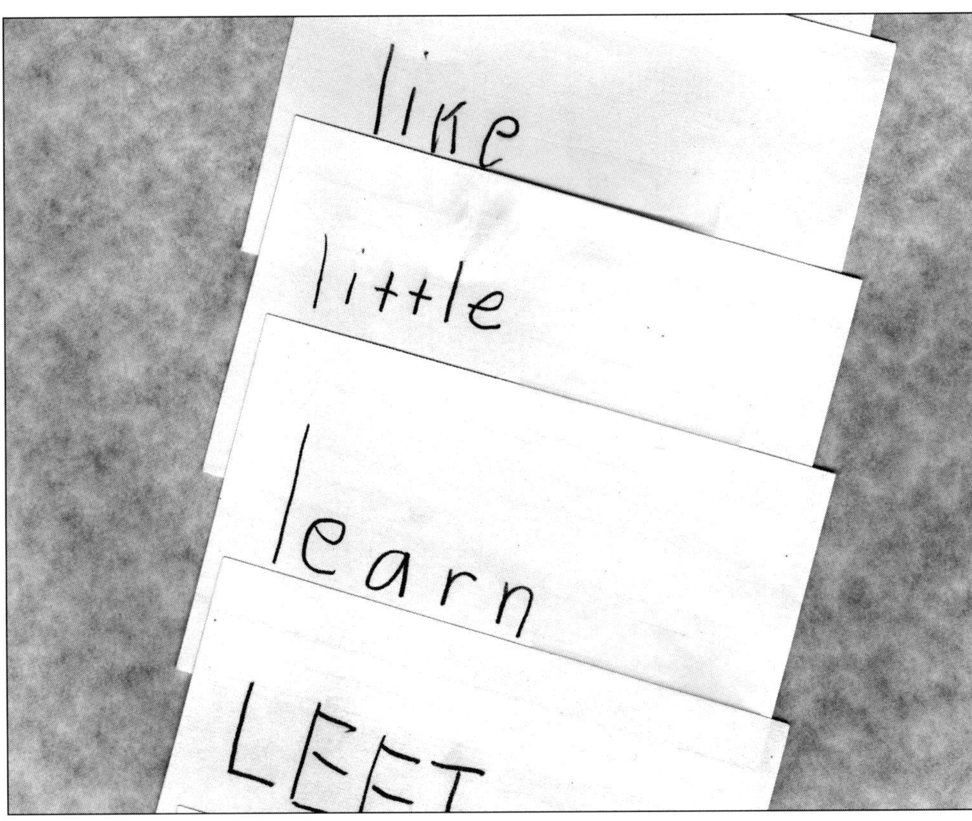

- Check each child's ability to recognize and print the letters. Create activities to send home daily for any child who is still having trouble.

- Build enthusiasm by treating the words as collectibles. Give children words or pictures for the files as rewards. Ask children to bring in a favorite word from home (one that a family member helps them write and illustrate) and add it to their folders. Set up a bank for children to trade or borrow words or pictures for their files.

- Use the files in your lessons. For example, try a hunt, asking each child to find all the animal words or pictures in their file that begin with "m" or all the toys that begin with "b." Have the children make an index sheet for their file, writing on it all the words they have that match the hunt's criteria. Pair the children up and let them find a few words they can trade with each other to copy into their file and put on their index sheet.

Have a different child each day help you pick something to read to the class.

- Gather many different kinds of written texts to choose from: a book (or part of one) from the class library or from home, a "wordy" comic book, an entry from a children's encyclopedia, the school lunch menu for the week, the weather report from the daily paper, an article from a children's magazine, the riddles from the Sunday comics, the Saturday morning listing from a TV guide, the monthly event calendar from the school or some other community organization, a menu from a local favorite restaurant, a recipe, a shopping list, a story written by a child, directions for playing a board game, a class roster, a report card form, a preprinted standardized test.

- Ask questions that will help the children discuss the meaning of what is read but also to notice the different structures and conventions. For example, you are supposed to get all the food items mentioned on a shopping list, but not on a menu! How do you know what day the 11:30 listing in the television guide is for? What kinds of printed material tell you who wrote it and where is this information shown? What's the same about a riddle and a test? What is different? Which kinds of printed materials are only a part of a whole, and how do you find that out? How does the table of contents work? What is supposed to be fact and what is fiction, and how do you tell?

Make a copy for each child of some text you have just read to the class, but put on the top a direction like "Find and underline all the words that use the letter 'w'." Give them a chance to talk about the different ways the letter is printed, noticing the differences between uppercase and lowercase and the different design or fonts that appear. Then, have the children circle the words that begin with the target letter and put their finished and corrected copies in their alphabet files for that letter, ready to be used for hunts and trades along with the other words in folder for that letter.

Decoding, Word Recognition, and Oral Reading

During first grade, the emphasis is on moving from pretend reading to conventional reading, relying less on others to read, and more on oneself. By the end of the year, every first grader should be able to read aloud with comprehension and reasonable fluency any text that is appropriately designed for the first grade, at least on a second reading. A book that is appropriately designed for the first half of first grade should be read with reasonable fluency and comprehension the first time through. By now, they are decoding accurately any phonetically regular one-syllable word, and they are able to rely on the alphabetic principle to attack unknown words. They also should be able to recognize common, irregularly spelled words by sight (e.g., "have," "said," "where," "two").

Across the days and weeks of the school year, there should be a clear plan for when new curriculum elements will be introduced—with sufficient time for intentional and intensive treatment by the first grade teacher. Just as important, children need ample time to explore and practice, so that what they have learned becomes easy and automatic.

Books and kits, as well as district-, school-, and teacher-made materials, offer many activities for first graders. As always, different children may be concentrating on different elements at different times. (The following are examples of valuable whole-class activities that can easily complement any teacher's approach to literacy instruction.)

Activities

Making Words—Give each child a set of 26 letter cards, with corresponding uppercase and lowercase letters printed on either side (vowels in red, consonants in black). Here's how to work with them:

1. You announce and display the letters for the day: one or two vowels and three or more consonants.

2. The children pull the same letters from their own set of cards.

3. Now you call out words for the children to make—at first a simple two-letter word, and then succeeding words with more letters. In this way, children practice spelling and reading 12 to 15 additional words each day. One at a time, the teacher displays the correctly spelled word, taking care to point out letter-sound correspondences and spelling patterns.

4. The highlight of this routine is the mystery word—one that the children must discover on their own by using all the preselected letters. As part of the activity, the teacher helps children explore new words, sorting by various spelling or phonetic features, such as word families, rhymes, common vowel and consonant combinations.

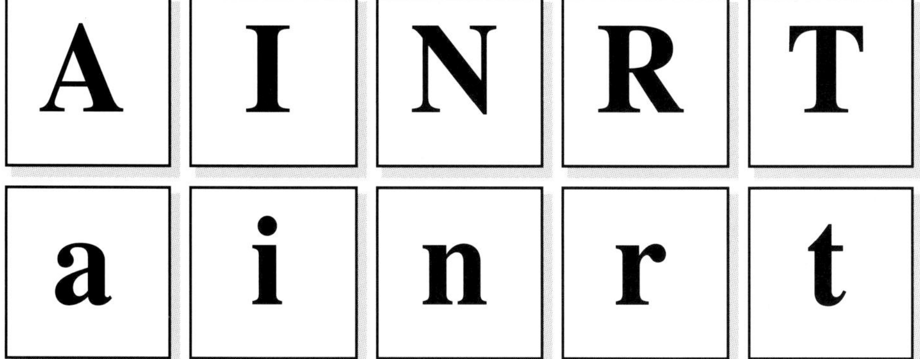

Call out words

an
in
at
rat
Nat
tan
tar
tin
ran
ant
art
rain

Mystery word:
train

Making words is a fun and engaging activity that also gives teachers the opportunity for explicit instruction on specific spelling-sound relationships and the alphabetic principle in general. As each new word is displayed, children can correct themselves by comparing their spelling with the teacher's. Struggling children benefit from working with a limited number of letters at one time. Also, the activity is inherently motivational: children at all levels can experience both success and instructional challenge as the lessons get more complex.

One study found that first grade children who used these activities showed significant improvement in their reading abilities. Some students were even able to read fifth and sixth grade passages. This is particularly noteworthy, since teachers and parents alike often worry that whole-class instruction will slow down higher-achieving students. This clearly need not be the case.

Word Wall—Select five words each week from a phonics lesson, a new book, or from the children's writing. These words are posted on the word wall and, as a whole group, the children practice reading and spelling them with daily chanting, clapping, and writing routines. Save time for the children to add the words to their alphabet files. New words are added weekly, maybe at the suggestion of different children.

Language, Comprehension, and Response to Text

By the middle of the school year, first graders should be readily talking and writing about new texts they are reading. They are learning how to summarize, how to locate the main ideas, and how to make connections, both factual and emotional, to life and to other reading. They are beginning to draw inferences from text—understanding what is not stated explicitly, why something is funny, and what will probably come next. In short, they are becoming readers—building an interest in various types of books, as well as increasing comfort with the ideas, information, enjoyment, and language that print can bring them in their everyday lives.

By the end of this year, first grade children should be reading and comprehending both fiction and nonfiction that is appropriately designed for first-grade level. They have an expanding language repertoire, and they should be spending at least 10 minutes reading aloud to someone each day.

Research shows that, with daily encouragement to read, practice, and enjoy books, students can improve their fluency, word recognition, and comprehension skills. They also gain motivation. For these purposes, children need high-quality materials, including a range of texts selected for their unique interests and abilities.

Activities

Give children the chance to thoroughly master more difficult texts through repeated readings. Most first graders love to read the same books over again, particularly if they are good ones, so don't be afraid of repetition.

- Choose books that children know and enjoy and set up various rereading arrangements such as whole-class, small-group, and individual rereading assignments. Remember to treat various small groups sensitively, depending on the ability of the students. For example, proficient readers can take turns reading parts of the book in a "round robin." A slower group can read an easier book "round robin" style, or a teacher or aide can read the same book aloud, letting the children take turns reading the last word of each sentence.

- You also may wish to send children home with a book to reread with a parent, older sibling, or other caregiver. So that the child has a trophy for her efforts, ask the caregiver to write a note back, for example, with comments about what he or she liked about it. The next day, during whole-class time, have the children do a choral reading. Ask them, "What did the people at home think of this story? Were you surprised at their reaction?" Draw them out on their impressions.

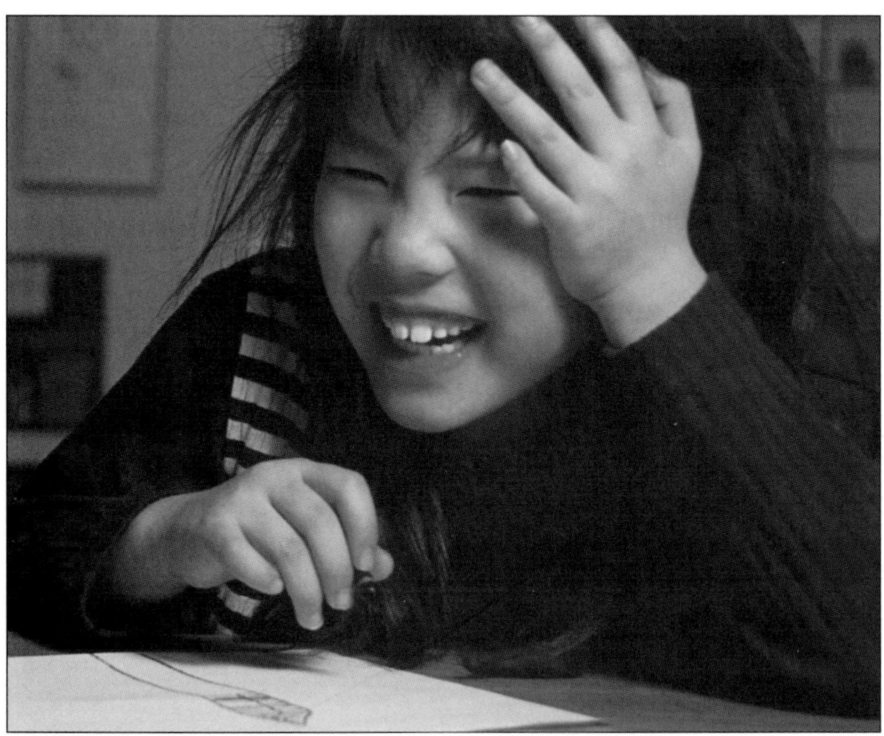

Bringing It All Together with Hot Cross Buns

"What does lukewarm mean?" asks Alex.

"Something that is between hot and cold," replies Ms. Cane.

"That's just plain warm. I want to know about lukewarm."

"Well, it's a special kind of warm . . ."

"Where is it on the thermometer?"

"Umm, well, really, you feel it on your skin and . . ."

"Why? and why not just say warm?"

Today is hot cross buns day in Ms. Cane's first grade class, and Ms. Cane loves it. She loves the controversy over the word "lukewarm." She loves the enthusiasm that the project stirs. And she loves the fact that in this single activity she can integrate so many of her first-grade reading goals. The recipe forces the children to explore syntax. It helps them build their vocabularies. It requires word attack strategies. It demands their comprehension. And finally, hot cross buns give the class a chance to work as a team on creating something wonderful together—all thanks to their reading skills.

Soon, the classroom looks something like a bakery. Ms. Cane has brought in a stack of cookbooks, measuring spoons and measuring cups, mixing bowls, flour, sugar, and other ingredients. The children are gathered around in a circle and each has a copy of the recipe. Some children have volunteered to read the ingredients, while others get to hold the cooking equipment, showing how they would carry out the recipe's instructions.

Not long after the class is resolved on the issue of "lukewarm" comes a spirited discussion about "flour" versus "flower." In both instances, Ms. Cane settles the issue to her satisfaction, but makes a note to herself that she must casually bring these words up again later to be sure that the children have understood.

Now it is Julie's turn to read a sentence of the recipe. "Beat throughly," she says.

Ms. Cane congratulates her on reading the word "beat" correctly. At her prompting, the class chants,

"When two vowels go a walking,
the first one does the talking."

"But Julie, let's take a look at the second word of that sentence," says Ms. Cane. "It's not 'thr' like in 'three.' Look more closely. There's a vowel between 'th' and 'r.' Ms. Cane reads the word "thoroughly" in the conventional way, exaggerating and slowing down the sounds. The class repeats it after her.

"Any idea what it means?"

The class offers a lot of guesses about beating speed, but finally, Julie says, "All the way through."

"Exactly!" praises Ms. Cane. "Now let's figure out what it means to beat something all the way through." The class now talks about mixing something so well that you can't see the separate ingredients.

One person misses this part of the discussion. It's Julie, who is looking away with a pout, quietly muttering "Throughly. Like I said. All the way through." She says it over and over, unwilling to let go of her original word.

A few minutes later, the class reads the recipe once again. This time, Julie says the word correctly.

About two hours later, Julie encounters the word again. This time she reads the word correctly, confiding to Ms. Cane, "The first time I saw this word, I thought it was like 'three.' But there's an 'o' before the 'r'. See?"

"Oh, very good, Julie," replies Ms. Cane, who graciously treats this as a new and valuable revelation.

Hot Cross Buns

2 packs active dry yeast	*3 1/2 cups flour*
1/3 cup lukewarm water	*1 teaspoon cinnamon*
1/3 cup warm milk	*3 eggs*
1/2 cup oil	*2/3 cup currants*
1/3 cup sugar	*1 egg white*
3/4 teaspoon salt	*1 cup special sugar*

Put the yeast in water until it gets soft. Meanwhile, mix together the milk, oil, sugar, and salt. Sift together the flour and cinnamon. Stir the flour mixture and the milk mixture together to make dough.

Crack the eggs. Beat thoroughly. Add eggs to the dough. Beat thoroughly again. Add yeast and currants to the dough. Cover up the bowl and put it in a warm place to rise until the dough is two times as big as it started . . . i

Surround class reading sessions with discussion and activities to help children develop their comprehension and vocabulary skills.

1. *Prereading Activity* Help children develop background knowledge and vocabulary they need to understand the text they are about to read. Find related text and information to share with them and have them do projects and other activities that will enrich their understanding of the concept, setting, or topic of the new text.

   Look for new, unusual words in a story and discuss them together. Ask children to use the new words in another sentence. Talk about words that are synonyms or antonyms of the new words. Ask, "Could you say the same thing another way?" "How would you say the opposite?" Put the new vocabulary words on your word wall or in the children's alphabet files.

2. *Reading* While the class is reading a story, be sure to orchestrate pauses for questions and discussion that will help comprehension.

- Make children feel comfortable enough to ask their own questions. Some of the conventions of written language can cause problems for a young reader. Imagine the child who has just learned to tell time and then encounters the sentence, "The family waited three long hours." "Isn't an hour always 60 minutes?" he asks. "How can one hour be any longer than another?" During the class reading, the teacher can take a moment to lead the children to explain that the author added the word "long" to tell us how the family felt while waiting. And yes, an hour always contains 60 minutes.

- Teachers don't have to hold off to the end of the story to ask their questions either. Help children build their comprehension skills by encouraging them to

—compare and contrast
For example, "Toad was worried about his garden. But how did Frog feel about it?"

—predict
For example, "What do you think Toad will do next?"

—ask why and how
For example, "Why did Frog and Toad want to tie up the cookies with string?" Or "Why did they give their cookies to the birds?"

—check their understanding of the sequence
"What happened after Toad woke up from his dream?"

The story takes plas outside.

3. *After Reading*

- Promote discussions that help children to

  —Summarize: discuss issues of plot and lead children to summarize what happened in the story. With children's input, make a list of all the plot points on the board. For nonfiction, make a list of all the major facts or ideas that the text contained.

  —Develop character understanding: ask questions about the motives, interests, and concerns of real or fictional characters in their texts. For example, "Even though Toad was doing great and wonderful things in his dream, he was unhappy. Why?" Children may answer, "Because he missed his friend, Frog." Help them to go further. Ask what this tells us about Toad. (That he is a character who cares about friendship more than glory.)

  —Relate texts to their own lives: encourage children to make connections between the texts and themselves, their homes, their neighborhoods, their feelings and aspirations. If children read an illustrated essay about animal tracks, ask them to talk about the animals and birds in their backyard or neighborhood, and what sort of tracks they might see. The discussion can go in many personal directions from here. You might ask children what traces they leave behind when they take a walk. Or the class might consider the lives of scientists who study animal tracks and whether or not this might be an interesting field of work.

- Give children a writing or drawing assignment connected to what they have read. They can do this in groups, in class, or at home. You might have children do a book review, or ask them to write a letter to the author, explaining any feelings or insights about the author's work. To get children started, ask them if they think the author expressed himself or herself very well and why. Ask if the story could have been improved and if there was something else they wish the author had added to his or her work.

  Another creative approach is to have students write and illustrate an advertisement about the book, designed to appeal to the next year's class. Ask the class if they think other children might like the book and why, and suggest that they include this information in their advertisement. Help them to come up with slogans and a dramatic or enticing scene from the book that would work well for illustration in their advertisement.

"Kids are natural question askers. But they don't always know how to ask the nitty gritty questions you need to ask to understand the meaning of literature. They'll ask superficial questions, like what color a character's dress was. With the reciprocal teaching approach, I model for them and show them the kinds of questions they need to ask. I might start with sequence, asking what happened first in a story. Then I move on to comparisons, asking what is similar or different between past stories and the one we're reading now. With fairy tales and nursery rhymes, I ask them to find similar themes. If you don't show them, they never learn. They need to hear it, see it, and try it themselves."

—Susan Derber
First grade teacher
Sandburg School
Springfield, Illinois

Spelling and Writing

By the end of the year, first graders should be correctly spelling three- and four-letter short vowel words. They are composing fairly readable first drafts, paying some attention to planning, drafting, basic punctuation, and correcting. Also, they are increasingly comfortable with a wide variety of writing formats: stories, descriptions, letters, and journal entries, as well as illustrations and graphics.

It is important for parents and teachers to understand that invented spelling is not in conflict with correct spelling. On the contrary, it plays an important role in helping children learn how to write. When children use invented spelling, they are in fact exercising their growing knowledge of phonemes, the letters of the alphabet, and their confidence in the alphabetic principle. A child's "iz" for the conventional "is" can be celebrated as quite a breakthrough! It is the kind of error that shows you that the child is thinking independently and quite analytically about the sounds of words and the logic of spelling.

Yes, first grade children should be expected to correctly spell previously studied words and spelling patterns in their final writing products. But experimenting with spelling in the primary grades provides an invaluable opportunity for new readers to understand and extend their lessons on letter-sound and sound-spelling relationships. The combination of invented spelling and well-designed instruction over time ensures that their independent spellings of new words will become increasingly correct even as it makes studied words easier to remember.

Activities

At the beginning of first grade, the challenge of writing something all by oneself is brand new to many children. Start them out with a topic that is familiar and manageable. Tell children they are going to write a book about themselves. Explain the concept of a work in progress, and provide each child with paper and a folder in which they will keep their work. Tell the students that, when all the pages are finished, they will put them together to make a book. Show them where you are keeping the files when they are not in use.

- Begin the first writing session by asking children what kinds of things might be in a book about themselves. Keep a running list on a large piece of paper that all can see. Their responses might include things they like to do, their favorite colors, favorite foods, their family, where they live, their pets, etc. When they are finished, tell them that you are going to put the list aside for future use.

- Now, tell children that they are going to create page one of their books and that, since this is a book about them, page one should say who they are. Have children draw a self-portrait—as detailed and personalized as possible. Then have them write their names beneath the drawing. You may wish to have the children discuss and share their pictures. At the end of this session, have children date their work and put it back in their files.

- On another day, take out the list that the children developed and read it back to the class, giving them the opportunity to add or change things. Now explain that today they are going to write another page in their "About Me" books. Let children choose anything they wish from the list. Once they have decided on an idea, they can begin writing or drawing.

- Continue in this way, over the course of several weeks, having the children work on a page at a time, chosen from their original list of topics. While they are busy writing, circulate around the class and give individual help in writing captions for pictures and spelling words. During some or all of the writing sessions, you may wish to invite a few children to share their work with one another and offer constructive responses to their classmates.

Tip: When the project is finished, you may wish to take an instant photograph of each child to paste on the front of their finished books. The books can make a good holiday present for someone in the child's family.

Yesterday my cat died.
Today at math we did a
math sheet. It was fun.
At art we panted a
pikcher. It was fun.
Then for Spanish we
colered. It was fun.

Sara - I am sorry about your cat.
I know she was very special to you.
I know exactly how you feel because
I have been through the same
thing.
She lived a wonderful long life
and she will always be in your heart.
She is now up in heaven.
If you need to talk about
it please know I am here for you.

Love,
miss Rohe

Have children write and read their own writing. Supply paper and writing utensils and invite children to write and illustrate their own stories. Have an author's chair ceremony to invite students to read and talk about their stories (or other genres such as reports, directions, and poems). A special classroom chair is designated as the author's chair—when a student sits in the author's chair, the other students sit in front of that child, ready and willing to listen to the child's writing. If children use invented spellings, ask them to explain how they figured out how to write one or two intriguing examples.

Develop dialogue or chitchat journals. Provide each child with a notebook (preferably a composition style notebook that won't lose its pages). Tell the children that these journals will give them the chance to tell you about anything they want. The only rules are that they must write at least two lines in their journals at least twice a week. They can write about their pets, their friends, their families, their favorite television shows. If they cannot think of anything to say, they still must write at least two lines, even if it is just "blah blah blah."

Tell the children that twice a week you will read what they have written and that you also will follow the rules and contribute at least two lines each time.

After they make an entry, have children drop off their journals at the front of class in a bag.

The children's writings offer a chance for you to learn about your students, their interests, and their emerging abilities as readers and writers. With the daily chitchat, you also have the chance to give them regular feedback and motivation to write. Use your responses to provoke an ongoing written dialogue about topics, ideas, and experiences. As time goes on, interesting exchanges will unfold.

Spelling words complements reading them. Choose a list of five words that match the letter-sound patterns the children currently are learning to read. Say the first word as part of a sentence. Then say it alone. Then say it very slowly, almost pausing between each sound. Now go to the board and call for the class to help you choose the letters you should write in order to spell it correctly. Do the same routine for each of the next words. Then have the class read the list from the board. Next, have each child take a piece of paper while you erase the board. Say the words, one by one, in a different order, but stop after each word to give the children a chance to write it. After everyone has written the first word, choose one child to go to the board, say it slowly, and write it. Give everyone a chance to fix their spelling before you go on to the next word. Ask the children to spell the words for someone at home that night. They should also ask that person at home to write down a sentence that the child has dictated for each of the five words, leaving a blank where the word should go. Next day, read the sentences from home and have the child fill in the blank.

Accomplishments of the First Grade Student

In first grade, it should all come together: language and literacy skills should combine to turn children into real readers. A particular set of accomplishments that the successful learner should exhibit by the end of first grade are shown in the following table. Because of their importance, we present them in full, as published in *Preventing Reading Difficulties in Young Children* (National Academy Press, 1998). Again, this list is neither exhaustive nor incontestable, but it does capture many highlights of the course of literacy acquisition. Although the timing of these accomplishments will vary among children, they are the sorts of things that should be in place when children enter second grade.

First Grade Accomplishments

- Makes a transition from emergent to "real" reading.
- Reads aloud with accuracy and comprehension any text that is appropriately designed for the first half of grade one.
- Accurately decodes orthographically regular, one-syllable words and nonsense words (e.g., "sit," "zot"), using print-sound mappings to sound out unknown words.
- Uses letter-sound correspondence knowledge to sound out unknown words when reading text.
- Recognizes common, irregularly spelled words by sight ("have," "said," "where," "two").
- Has a reading vocabulary of 300 to 500 sight words and easily sounded-out words.
- Monitors own reading and self-corrects when an incorrectly identified word does not fit with cues provided by the letters in the word or the context surrounding the word.
- Reads and comprehends both fiction and nonfiction that is appropriately designed for the grade level.
- Shows evidence of expanding language repertoire, including increasing appropriate use of standard, more formal language.
- Creates own written texts for others to read.
- Notices when difficulties are encountered in understanding text.
- Reads and understands simple written instructions.
- Predicts and justifies what will happen next in stories.
- Discusses prior knowledge of topics in expository texts.
- Uses how, why, and what-if questions to discuss nonfiction texts.
- Describes new information gained from texts in own words.
- Distinguishes whether simple sentences are incomplete or fail to make sense; notices when simple texts fail to make sense.
- Can answer simple written comprehension questions based on the material read.
- Can count the number of syllables in a word.
- Can blend or segment the phonemes of most one-syllable words.
- Spells correctly three- and four-letter short vowel words.
- Composes fairly readable first drafts using appropriate parts of the writing process (some attention to planning, drafting, rereading for meaning, and some self-correction).
- Uses invented spelling or phonics-based knowledge to spell independently, when necessary.
- Shows spelling consciousness or sensitivity to conventional spelling.
- Uses basic punctuation and capitalization.
- Produces a variety of types of compositions (e.g., stories, descriptions, journal entries) showing appropriate relationships between printed text, illustrations, and other graphics.
- Engages in a variety of literacy activities voluntarily (e.g., choosing books and stories to read, writing a note to a friend).

Directions for Second and Third Grades

On opening day of second grade, teachers typically face two sets of students: those who read well independently and those who appear not to know how to read at all. Most of the second group seem to have forgotten—during a summer with no reading practice—what they learned during the first grade. Others failed to learn properly in the first place. As quickly as possible, the second grade teacher's job is to figure out which children are which and to ensure that all gain or regain the first grade accomplishments.

A major task, then, is to ensure that all students understand the alphabetic principle—and then move on. Teachers can start with short regular words such as "pot," "pan," and "pat," moving on to more complex patterns and words, always with the goal of helping children see the larger logic and regularities of the alphabetic system at work. In third grade, this instruction should extend to spellings and meanings of prefixes, suffixes, and root words.

Beyond securing, or resecuring, these skills, the second and third grade curricula have two major goals:

* to help children build automatic word recognition, spelling skills, and reading fluency.

* to improve comprehension by building knowledge of words, language structures, attitudes, and conscious strategies required for understanding and using text.

The main goal of this book is to help prevent reading difficulties in young children. For this reason, emphasis has been given to the prekindergarten years, kindergarten, and first grade—a formative and influential time for language, literacy, and reading development.

Certainly, the kinds of activities described in previous sections of this book should be continued and integrated into existing teaching materials—and adapted to the needs of students. In particular, students who are still struggling with the alphabetic principle and decoding skills will benefit from activities described in the first grade section—with adaptations and content for second or third grade.

However, by the time children reach second grade, they have already built up personal histories of successes or failures with reading. In addition, teachers are well into a district-mandated curriculum or published program, and they are expected to continue with the scope and sequence that they have started. For these reasons, it is more difficult for us to offer broad generalizations about what teachers should and shouldn't be doing. That is why this section does not

contain specific activities for second and third graders. Rather, we provide an overview of accomplishments for second and third graders. Certainly it is not exhaustive. Rather than a checklist of milestones, we offer parents and teachers a general direction for instruction and development.

"At the beginning of the year, many of my students feel nervous and worried about reading. They think that they're not good readers because they've struggled with decoding and phonics. I work on making it fun. Instead of reading groups, we have book clubs. I change the grouping frequently. At times, I make groups based on ability so that I can focus on kids who need help. But I don't keep kids stuck with the same people all the time. Also, sometimes kids push themselves a little harder when they hear someone who reads a little better. And we have rules in our book clubs: you must always be nice; you can't interrupt; you have to follow along. Then everyone feels comfortable, even if the abilities are mixed."

"Most of the work I do on fluency happens during these sessions when it's just three or four of us in a group. There are times when I pick the book, but there are other times when I give them choices. That gets them more involved, because they feel more empowered. My experience is that the more interested they are, the more they want to read. That's when I see improved comprehension."

"As new readers, children can become so focused on reading clearly and sounding out the words. But you ask them a question and they don't know what they've read. Once they realize that this is a fun book club and that at the end we're going to do a project on what the book is about, then they start thinking about the meaning—what's funny about the book, what we can say about it. Then they start to understand. They learn that you read because you are trying to make sense of the text. You're not just reading these isolated words. You're reading to get meaning."

—Valorie Burgess
Second grade teacher
The Children's Learning Center
Rockville, MD

Strategies for Comprehension and Fluency

If children are to move ahead and read independently at the next level, they need practice, reading and rereading, in both fluency and comprehension skills. One ambitious study of 14 second grade classrooms reorganized the curriculum to give students strategies for understanding text and a great deal of practice to build fluency. i

After reading each text selection aloud, the teacher discussed it with the class and taught vocabulary. For comprehension building, she used story maps, plot charts, and diagrams to help students analytically explore the meaning of the selection. Each student then read the selection again at home, preferably aloud to a parent. The next day, students read passages once again from the same text, this time to one another in pairs. In addition, children wrote in their journals and read books of their own choice for 15 to 20 minutes each day at school and at home. The results were quite positive: children showed significant growth in their reading skills across the school year.

Words and Knowledge

Can teachers improve their students' word knowledge and comprehension through instruction? The answer is yes. Vocabulary instruction does create measurable increases in students' word knowledge. But how we go about it makes all the difference. Teaching specific words may improve children's knowledge of those particular words taught—but that is all it does. It is important to explore new words and concepts at every opportunity and to revisit them frequently, enriching their usage and meaning. It is also important to develop the children's inclination to notice and learn about new words they encounter on their own while reading. In addition, they also build their vocabularies through reading. As stated throughout this book, kids need to read every day, both in and out of school.

"Even children with limited comprehension skills will build vocabulary and cognitive structures through immersion in literacy activities. An encouraging message for teachers of low-achieving children is implicit here. We often despair of changing 'abilities,' but there is at least one partially malleable habit that will itself develop 'abilities'—reading."

—Keith Stanovich
Researcher
Ontario Institute for the Study of Education
Toronto, Ontario

Comprehension Techniques

Children can learn to monitor their own reading process and develop better comprehension skills. Explicitly teaching children to use conscious strategies is effective, according to several studies, particularly with children at risk. One example is a method called reciprocal teaching, which focuses on an exchange of turns in dialogues between teachers and students. i

Outstanding Teachers

Probably the single most important factor in a child's initial reading instruction is his or her teacher. No books, no curriculum, no computer can replace the enormous value of good human-to-human teaching.

What are the characteristics of excellent teaching?

One recent observational and survey study examined the literacy instruction of 123 primary teachers who were described as "outstanding" by their schools.

i One thing these teachers had in common was an effective and deliberate plan to offer instruction that meets the diverse needs of their students. In their classrooms, they made it a point to

- create a literate environment in which the children have access to a variety of reading and writing materials;
- present intentional instruction for reading and writing, using trade books and other literature and providing practice using games and activities separate from connected text;
- carefully choose instructional-level text from a variety of materials, with a reliance on literature, big books, and linking reading and writing activities;
- create multiple opportunities for sustained reading practice in a variety of formats, such as choral, individual, and partner reading;
- adjust the intensity of instruction to meet the needs of individual students;
- encourage children to consciously monitor their understanding; and
- competently manage activities, behavior, and classroom resources.

In reciprocal teaching, teachers give children practice in four strategies: predicting, questioning, summarizing, and clarifying. Children and adults take turns leading discussions about the text. The goal is not only to practice the strategies, but ultimately to come to conclusions about the meaning of the passage read. In the reciprocal teaching model, the text has content that can spur discussions. It is also centered on themes that, over time, build children's knowledge of a topic. When they are first learning these techniques, teachers give a lot of guidance.

Reciprocal teaching has been studied mainly for its effects on high-risk children—with positive results. First and second grade students have shown significant improvement in listening comprehension, as well as fewer referrals to special education and remedial programs. In addition, teachers reported that children who previously appeared to have a disability functioned quite well during the reciprocal teaching sessions.

What Happens in Second Grade

Decoding, Word Recognition, and Oral Reading

By the end of second grade, children should be able to read and comprehend both fiction and nonfiction that is appropriately designed for their grade level. They are accurately decoding phonetically regular, two-syllable words and nonsense words. They are using their phonics knowledge to sound out unknown words, including multisyllable words. And they are rapidly gaining the ability to read the longer, more complex sentences of written language with fluency and expression.

Language, Comprehension, and Response to Text

Children should be motivated enough to read voluntarily for their own interests and purposes. They should read to find out answers to their questions and be well acquainted with the purposes of many different print resources, such as dictionaries, atlases, chapter books, weather reports—even joke books. They are

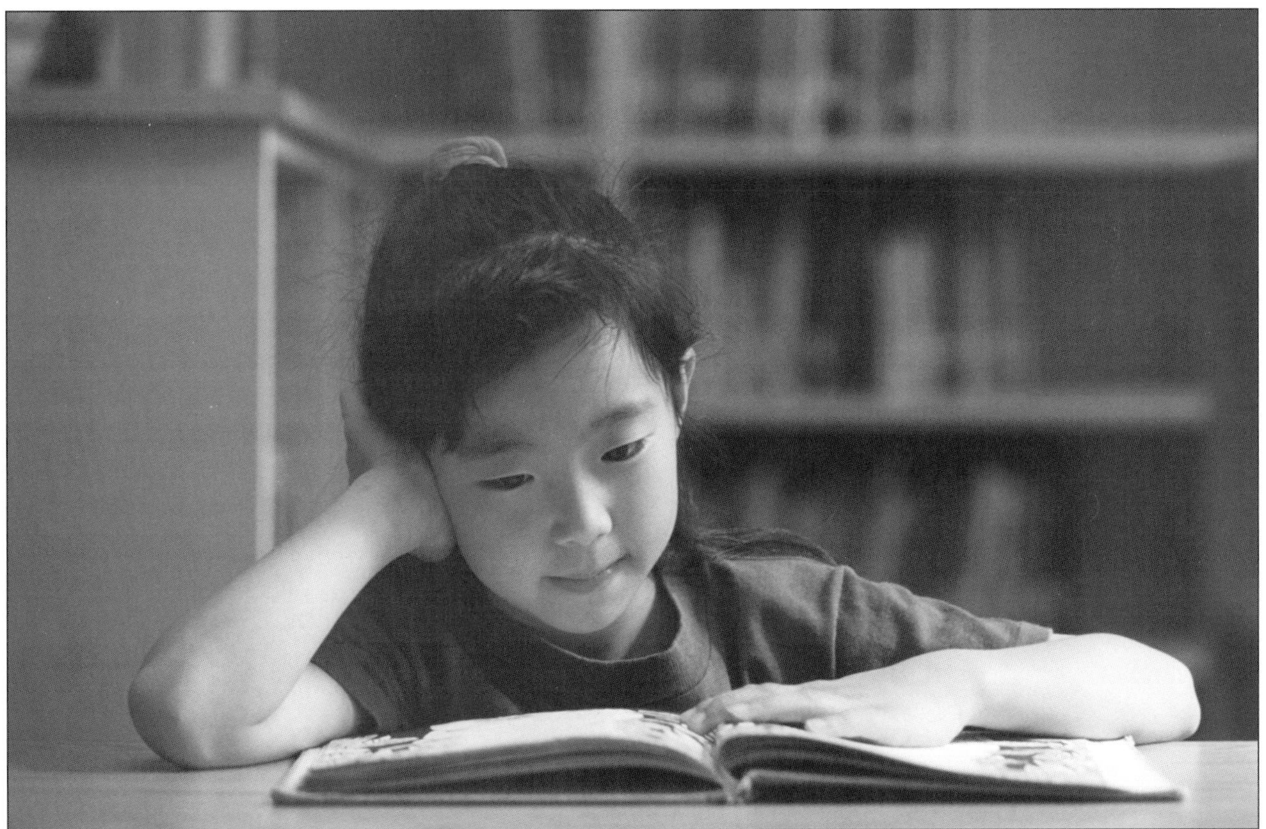

reading independently every day, outside school. In their speech and writing, they are showing an expanding repertoire of language and vocabulary.

Second graders should also be busily learning how to learn from text. They are interpreting information from diagrams, charts, and graphs, and they recall facts and details. They are participating in creative responses to texts, such as dramatizations, oral presentations, and fantasy play. They are comparing and contrasting characters and events across stories and offer answers to how, why, and what-if questions in nonfiction texts. They are explaining and describing new concepts and information in their own words. They can identify parts of speech such as nouns, verbs, adjectives, and adverbs.

Spelling and Writing

In second grade, children should be correctly spelling most previously studied words and spelling patterns. When spelling a new word, they are representing all the sounds, even if they are still spelling some of those sounds inconsistently. They are rapidly incorporating the spelling patterns of the words they have studied into new words they attempt. Increasingly, they are becoming writers, using formal language patterns, such as quotes and proper verb forms, in their writing products. They are making reasonable judgments about what to include when they write, and they are now able to productively discuss how to revise, edit, and refine a piece of writing. With some organizational help, they are writing informative, well-structured reports. In the process, they are attending to spelling, mechanics, and presentation for final products, which may include a wide variety of formats, such as short stories, research report, and letters. When they have it available, students at this age are using computer technology for composition and presentations.

In math I learned bar graghs.

gragh
tally marks
bar gragh
organizes info.
easy to read
pichograph
information

What Happens in Third Grade

Decoding, Word Recognition, and Oral Reading

By the end of third grade, students should be reading aloud with fluency and comprehension any text that is appropriately designed for the first half of third grade. They should also be able to read any third grade text, fiction or nonfiction, with understanding. They should have the independent control to reread sentences when necessary. They should notice words, language, or concepts that they don't understand on their own so that they can find out about them, typically by asking. They are increasingly comfortable at using letter-sound correspondences and structural analysis of prefixes and suffixes to decode unfamiliar words.

Language, Comprehension, and Response to Text

Most third graders are reading long fiction and chapter books independently, ideally at least 20 minutes every day outside school. During class, they are taking part in creative responses to texts, such as dramatizations, oral presentations, and fantasy play. In their speech and writing, they are demonstrating

new vocabulary and language. They are also using resources to get the information they need (e.g., table of contents, index, dictionary, and available technology).

Increasingly in the third grade, children are learning to read and learn from nonfiction texts. They are summarizing major points and discussing details. They can distinguish cause and effect. They can identify the main idea and supporting details of a text. With information and reasoning, they are examining the bases of hypotheses and opinions.

As roots, prefixes, and suffixes are taught in class, they are learning how to take words apart to infer their meanings. Not only are they now able to identify specific words or wordings that are causing them difficulties, they are increasingly able to use comprehension strategies and surrounding information in the text to infer or enrich their understanding of a new word or concept.

Spelling and Writing

Third graders should be producing a variety of written work, such as critical essays, reports, and their own "published" books. Their writing is now beginning to take on sophisticated language patterns, such as elaborate descriptions, figurative language, and dialogue. When producing reports, they are able to combine and write information from multiple sources, but they often need help in paraphrasing and, certainly, in giving credit for sources. During class sharing periods, they are presenting and discussing one another's writing with helpful suggestions and responses. With assistance, they are reviewing, editing, revising, and clarifying their own writing, including attention to spelling, mechanics, and presentation. Previously studied words and spelling patterns appear correctly in their finished products.

Accomplishments of the Second and Third Grade Student

Sets of accomplishments that the successful learner should exhibit by the end of second and third grades are shown in the following tables. Because of their importance, we present them in full as published in *Preventing Reading Difficulties in Young Children* (National Academy Press, 1998). Again, these lists are neither exhaustive nor incontestable, but they do capture many highlights of the course of literacy acquisition. Although the timing of these accomplishments will vary among children, they are the sorts of things that should be in place before entering the next grade.

Second Grade Accomplishments

- Reads and comprehends both fiction and nonfiction that is appropriately designed for grade level.
- Accurately decodes orthographically regular, multisyllable words and nonsense words (e.g., capital, Kalamazoo).
- Uses knowledge of print-sound mappings to sound out unknown words.
- Accurately reads many irregularly spelled words and such spelling patterns as diphthongs, special vowel spellings, and common word endings.
- Reads and comprehends both fiction and nonfiction that is appropriately designed for the grade.
- Shows evidence of expanding language repertory, including increasing use of more formal language registers.
- Reads voluntarily for interest and own purposes.
- Rereads sentences when meaning is not clear.
- Interprets information from diagrams, charts, and graphs.
- Recalls facts and details of texts.
- Reads nonfiction materials for answers to specific questions or for specific purposes.
- Takes part in creative responses to texts such as dramatizations, oral presentations, fantasy play, etc.
- Discusses similarities in characters and events across stories.
- Connects and compares information across nonfiction selections.
- Poses possible answers to how, why, and what-if questions.
- Correctly spells previously studied words and spelling patterns in own writing.
- Represents the complete sound of a word when spelling independently.
- Shows sensitivity to using formal language patterns in place of oral language patterns at appropriate spots in own writing (e.g., de-contextualizing sentences, conventions for quoted speech, literary language forms, proper verb forms).
- Makes reasonable judgments about what to include in written products.
- Productively discusses ways to clarify and refine own writing and that of others.
- With assistance, adds use of conferencing, revision, and editing processes to clarify and refine own writing to the steps of the expected parts of the writing process.
- Given organizational help, writes informative, well-structured reports.
- Attends to spelling, mechanics, and presentation for final products.
- Produces a variety of types of compositions (e.g., stories, reports, correspondence).

Third Grade Accomplishments

- Reads aloud with fluency and comprehension any text that is appropriately designed for grade level.
- Uses letter-sound correspondence knowledge and structural analysis to decode words.
- Reads and comprehends both fiction and nonfiction that is appropriately designed for grade level.
- Reads longer fictional selections and chapter books independently.
- Takes part in creative responses to texts such as dramatizations, oral presentations, fantasy play, etc.
- Can point to or clearly identify specific words or wordings that are causing comprehension difficulties.
- Summarizes major points from fiction and nonfiction texts.
- In interpreting fiction, discusses underlying theme or message.
- Asks how, why, and what-if questions in interpreting nonfiction texts.
- In interpreting nonfiction, distinguishes cause and effect, fact and opinion, main idea and supporting details.
- Uses information and reasoning to examine bases of hypotheses and opinions.
- Infers word meaning from taught roots, prefixes, and suffixes.
- Correctly spells previously studied words and spelling patterns in own writing.
- Begins to incorporate literacy words and language patterns in own writing (e.g., elaborates descriptions; uses figurative wording).
- With some guidance, uses all aspects of the writing process in producing own compositions and reports.
- Combines information from multiple sources in writing reports.
- With assistance, suggests and implements editing and revision to clarify and refine own writing.
- Presents and discusses own writing with other students and responds helpfully to other students' compositions.
- Independently reviews work for spelling, mechanics, and presentation.
- Produces a variety of written work (e.g., literature response, reports, "published" books, semantic maps) in a variety of formats including multimedia forms.

Computers in Classrooms and at Home

Recent advances in computer technology offer new support for reading instruction. Digitized and high-quality synthetic speech has been incorporated into programs focusing on phonological awareness and issues related to emergent literacy. These include letter-name and letter-sound knowledge, phonological decoding, spelling, and support for word decoding and comprehension while reading and writing stories. Computer speech, along with interesting graphics, animation, and speech recording, has supported the development of programs that are entertaining and motivating for both prereaders and beginning readers.

Talking books, widely distributed on CD-ROM, are among the most popular programs that claim to improve children's reading. Book pages are presented on the computer screen, and children can select the whole text or specific words and phrases to be read aloud by the computer. The most popular products include many clever animations that are highly entertaining to children, perhaps so much so that they distract from the task of reading; children can often access the animations without paying any attention to the print.

Storybook software displays storybooks on the screen. The programs come not only with software but also with ordinary printed material available for use without a computer. Some are stand-alone titles, such as *Living Books* and *Discuss* books. Others are parts of larger sets, such as IBM's *Stories* and More and Josten's *Dragontales*.

Multimedia writing tools motivate children to talk with each other about their composing acts and their final compositions. Children integrate previously prepared background illustrations, their own drawings, and writing into either stand-alone papers or multimedia slide shows.

IBM's *Writing to Read* program set the stage for classroom use of comprehensive literacy software programs for use in beginning reading instruction. The development of comprehensive literacy software for preprimary and primary-grade literacy has been accelerating, together with the more recent surge in the power/cost ratio of desktop computers. Comprehensive literacy software programs that have been developed more recently and for which systematic evaluation has begun include *Foundations in Learning* by Breakthrough to Literacy, *Early Reading Program* by Waterford, and the *Little Planet Literacy Series* by Young Children's Literacy Project.

Software

In recent years the consumer and school markets have become deluged with software products for children—products of dramatically varying quality. Following are examples of highly rated programs for children in the beginning elementary school years. These were rated for content, user friendliness, adult management features, strength of support materials, and value for the cost, rather than being examined for outcomes on children's learning.

Program	Brief Description
The Treehouse	The program addresses a number of skill areas. In terms of literacy, one activity is the construction of sentences with characters acting out the sentence upon completion.
Reader Rabbit 2	Provides young readers with practice in alphabetizing, rhyming, identifying long and short vowel sounds, and creating compound words.
My Own Stories	Provides students with word-processing, color graphics, sound effects, and music for use in creating their own stories. Stories can be printed.

Excellence in Primary Grade Teaching—A Career-Long Process

Excellent teaching is one of the most effective means in preventing reading difficulties. A recent study of more than 1,000 school districts found that every additional dollar spent on developing the qualifications of teachers netted improvements in student achievement greater than any other use of school resources. Yet districts currently spend less than one half of one percent of their resources on staff development.

Teacher education must be viewed in a new way: as a career-long undertaking, rather than something that is completed with the receipt of a bachelor's or

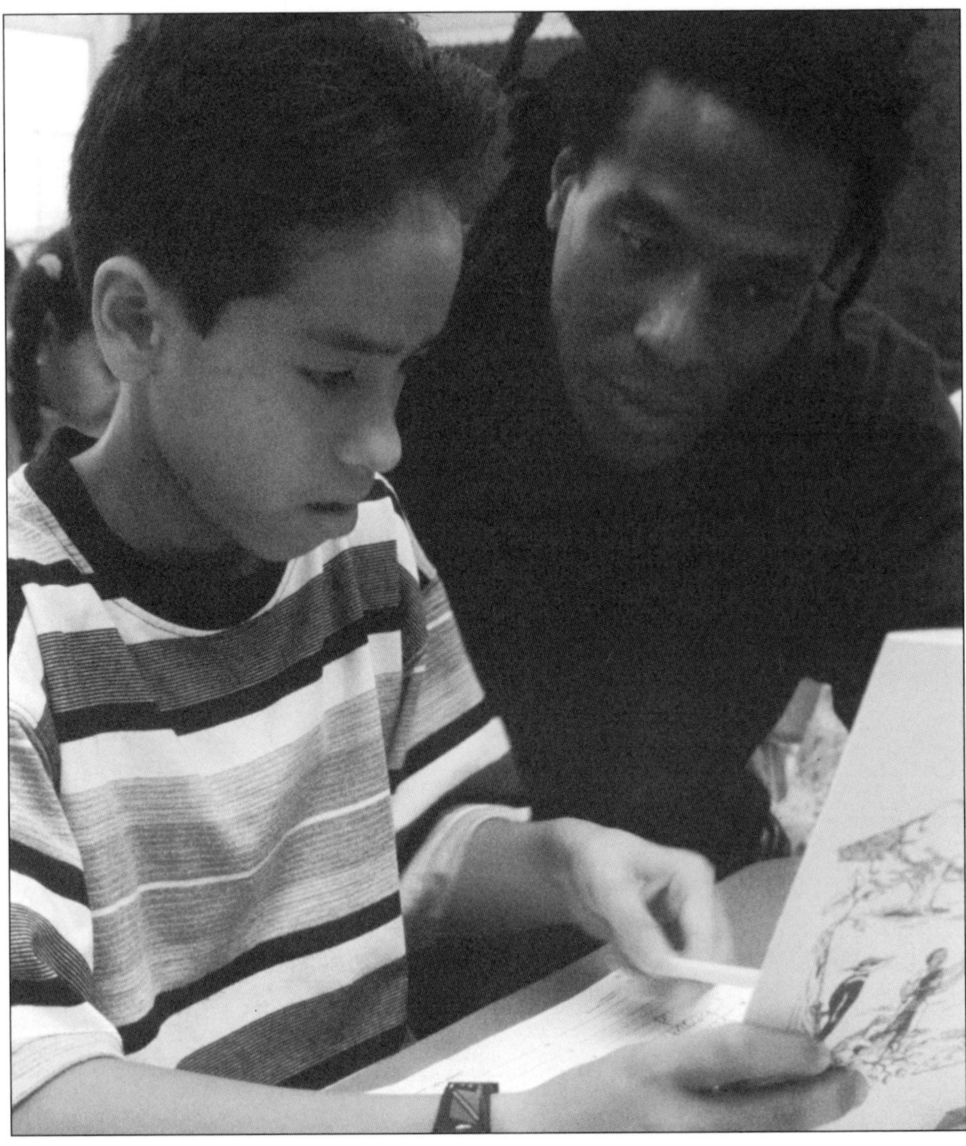

master's degree. Even the best undergraduate or graduate education program cannot fully prepare teachers for the complex process of teaching reading and the diverse needs they will face in their classrooms.

Reading is a complex process and to deal with it, teachers must have a strong background in cognitive behavioral and social sciences as well as in the humanities. Specific pedagogical knowledge and skills must be built from this base. Primary grade teachers must know a great deal about children's development, how they learn, and what they can do. They must be able to see students' strengths and weaknesses. They must plan good lessons to help students progress. And they must have a huge array of teaching techniques in their toolboxes in order to meet the vastly different needs of their students. In addition to all this, they must have content knowledge in literature, math, and science.

Teachers need to be knowledgeable about the scientific foundations of reading. Beyond this, a critical component in the preparation of primary grade teachers before they begin their careers is supervised, relevant, field experience in which they receive ongoing guidance and feedback. A principal goal of this experience is to achieve the ability to integrate and apply the knowledge learned in practice. Collaborative support by the teacher preparation institution and the field placement supervising teacher is essential. A critical component for novice teachers is the support of mentor teachers with excellent records of success in teaching reading that results in improved student outcomes.

It is absolutely essential that teachers at all grade levels understand the course of literacy development and the role of instruction in optimizing it. State certification requirements and teacher education curricula should be changed to incorporate this knowledge base, including, at a minimum:

- information about language development as it relates to literacy;
- information about the relationship between early literacy behavior and conventional reading;
- information about the features of an alphabetic writing system and other writing systems;
- information about both phonology and morphology in relation to spelling;
- information about comprehension and its dependence on other aspects of reading and on language skills;
- information about phonological awareness, orthographic awareness, and writing development;
- procedures for ongoing, in-class assessment of children's reading abilities;
- information on how to interpret and modify instruction according to norm-referenced and individually referenced assessment outcomes, including both formal and informal in-class assessments and progress-monitoring measures used by specialists;

- information about the learning and curricular needs of diverse learners (students with disabilities, with limited English proficiency, with English language dialect differences);
- in settings in which children are learning to read in a language other than English, an understanding of—as well as strategies and techniques for—teaching children to read in that language and information about bilingual language and literacy development;
- information on the design features and requirements of a reading curriculum;
- information about how teachers apply research judiciously to their practice, how to update their research knowledge, and how to influence research agendas, including teacher-researcher collaborations; and
- information about how to maintain and promote motivation to read and positive attitudes toward reading.

Thorough teacher education is essential; even so, teachers cannot possibly be fully prepared before the first day on the job. School districts should do more to encourage the ongoing, career-long development of teachers. Young teachers need support from mentor teachers as they develop. Experienced teachers should receive periodic training opportunities. Beyond traditional workshops, districts and schools should consider teacher research projects, discussion groups, school-university partnerships, and ways to encourage individual teacher efforts toward improvement (e.g., certification by the National Board for Professional Teacher Standards). In addition, schools should identify, reward, and acknowledge teachers who are highly effective, from the preschool level up.

Preventing Reading Difficulties

Most children who rely on schooling to learn to read and who receive good reading instruction do, in fact, become successful, lifelong readers. However, there are some children for whom good instruction is necessary—but not enough.

There are three stumbling blocks that are most likely to throw children off course on the journey to skilled reading:

1. Failure to understand or use the alphabetic principle, that is, the idea that written spellings systematically represent the sounds of spoken words in reading and writing.
2. Failure to acquire and use comprehension skills and strategies to get meaning from text.
3. Lack of fluency.

These three can combine to decrease children's motivation for learning how to read.

All over the United States, countless interventions strive to help children who are doing poorly in reading. In tutoring sessions, special education classes, free book programs, family literacy projects, and remedial instruction, there are educators, paraprofessionals, and volunteers who are trying to help struggling children to catch up.

Provided that they are designed to help children learn what they need to learn, programs with vastly different approaches show positive results. For this reason, a wide array of interventions are featured in this chapter, including tutoring, "pull-out" remediation programs, and dramatic school restructuring. Reading is an accomplishment that depends not just on discrete skills, but on a wide range of developmental supports and cognitive achievements. Mending an early language link is not by itself likely to have any effect on word reading if other connections in the net are frayed. Because reading is such a complex activity, children need an environment offering rich support and varied learning opportunities for every successive stage of their literacy development.

"Every week I send home a letter telling parents what we've done in the class. At the end of the letter, I give them a list of questions to ask the kids to check their comprehension. A lot of my parents would never ask these questions otherwise. When weeks go by and I don't get any letters back from a family, experience leads me to suspect that maybe the parents can't read themselves. Then I know that this child is going to need more of my time. I know that this child is out there alone."

—Ethelyn Hamilton-Frezel
Kindergarten teacher
Dr. Ronald E. McNair Elementary School
New Orleans, Louisiana

Some children are far more likely than others to have difficulties in learning to read. This may seem a simple and obvious fact. Yet it is a fact that is overlooked far too often.

If our goal is to ensure that all children in America can read, then we must target prevention efforts to the children who we know will need them the most. We must do this as early as possible—before children fail in school, before they are labeled, and before costly remediation is necessary.

What Makes a Good Reading Program?

In the early grades, the best reading programs offer a balance of elements, including reading for meaning and experiences with high-quality literature; intense, intentional, and systematic instruction in phonics; and ample opportunities to read and write. However, many commercial programs neglect certain aspects of instruction. Although most programs support activities that build comprehension, they may not include sufficient instruction in fluency, writing, and the alphabetic principle.

What does a well-balanced program look like? One example is a commercial program that offers a well-integrated approach using three distinct phases of instruction over the course of first grade.

During phase one, students develop phonemic awareness, the alphabetic principle, and a general understanding of how print works. A variety of games and activities give students practice in letter recognition, oral blending, and segmentation. For example, the teacher may ask "What rhymes with 'hat' and starts with 'c'?" Or, "Which of the following words begin with the letter 'n'?" To help children become knowledgeable about print, teachers read to them using big books and also encourage them to write every day. With language games and activities, the class also works on basic sight recognition of easy high-frequency words such as "the," "of," "you," "is," and "are."

During the second phase of the program, teachers explicitly teach letter-sound correspondences and spelling conventions. For the first time, children read independently with a graduated series of books that reinforce vocabulary and phonics lessons to date. As a part of their new reading efforts, they learn the strategy: if you don't recognize a word, sound it out.

Meanwhile, teachers connect phonics and spelling skills with dictation writing activities. Read-aloud sessions with big books include a variety of fiction and nonfiction centered on building knowledge on a topic children can enjoy. The program offers activities and books that engage children in exploration and the delights of literature.

By midyear, children move into the third phase of the program. They receive anthologies, with each unit focused on an explorable concept, such as animals and gardening. Teachers encourage children to compare selections in the units, in search of connections and overlapping themes. During guided reading sessions, they help children work on strategies, such as predicting, summing up, using context clues to understand words, making inferences, and articulating their personal responses. Individual and small groups of children work on projects, such as composing plays, puppet shows, and research reports. Phonics work now moves to more complex patterns, such as diphthongs, inflections, and polysyllabic words. Daily writing and reading sessions continue, as children move from decodable books to easy-to-read books and other stories that each can choose individually.

Who Are the Children Who Have Reading Difficulties?

Children Who Attend a Chronically Low-Achieving School

In a school that produces large numbers of children who cannot read at grade level, year after year, it is not necessary to assess children individually. We already know that children who attend this school are being placed at risk for reading difficulties. In these cases, teachers and principals should probably consider addressing the problem with system-wide restructuring and change, rather than invest in a costly child-by-child remediation process. Good teaching and a good classroom reading program can bring most students up to or near grade level during the primary grades. But sustaining this accomplishment is difficult when a large percentage of a school's students are failing.

Central to this restructuring is the need for effective reading instruction. A large number of students, who should be capable of reading ably given adequate instruction, are not doing so, suggesting that the instruction available is not appropriate. If the instruction provided by the school is ineffective or insufficient, many children will have difficulty learning to read (unless additional instruction is provided in the home or elsewhere). Children whose reading difficulties arise when the design of regular classroom curriculum, or its delivery, is flawed are sometimes termed curriculum casualties.

Children with Low English Proficiency

Hispanic students in the United States are at especially high risk. Despite progress over the past 15 to 20 years, they are about twice as likely as non-Hispanic whites to read well below average for their age. Many of these children also have parents who are poorly educated, come from low-income families, live in low-income communities, and attend low-achieving schools. With multiple risk factors in place, we can predict that, without excellent instruction, large numbers of these children will be at risk for reading difficulties.

Despite various controversies, considerable evidence suggests that limited or non-English-speaking language learners are generally more likely to become betters readers of English when they receive initial instruction in their native language.

Spoken language must come before written language; it is extremely hard to read a language that still is incomprehensible to the ear. Some language-minority children arrive at school with no proficiency in English, but speaking a different language for which there are instructional guides, learning materials, and locally available proficient teachers. These children should be taught the basics of reading in their native language while acquiring oral proficiency in English, and they

Reforming the System: Low-Achieving Schools

"We all realized that trying to fix a broken system was not the answer," says Jerry Allen, principal of Lackland City Elementary School in San Antonio, Texas. "We worked year after year using our regular reading curriculum, but we were never satisfied with the results. We would tweak it here and change it there. But it was the same basal adoption curriculum. I saw teacher after teacher hit the wall," recounts Allen, who describes his students as predominantly Hispanic and low-income. "After several years, you get to the point that you say 'I know I'm a bright person. I'm working very very hard, but my students are not progressing as they should.' And it is there that you slide down into a sea of mediocrity."

Allen's school put together a committee of 10 people whose sole responsibility for that year was to investigate reading programs that were successfully serving economically disadvantaged children. After combing through research, the committee got interested in a reading program that called for dramatic restructuring. Eventually they convinced the entire faculty to give it a try.

With a green light from the school's superintendent and a unanimous vote by teachers, the new program came to Lackland City Elementary School. Reading teachers put aside their old methods and wiped the slate clean.

Since launching the program three years ago, the school's average reading scores have risen across the board by about 15 percent each year. Currently the average reading scores are in the 72nd percentile, up from the mid-40th percentile.

"We kind of adopted the philosophy that, no matter what we do, our children must read. They can't be successful at mathematics and social studies if they can't read. Reading became our primary goal," says Allen. "I told my teachers that those 90 minutes of reading class was sacred time."

Allen claims that teacher training produces the greatest impact. "Rather than having a couple of reading specialists work with the bottom quartile of students, all the teachers on campus are now master reading teachers working with 100 percent of the students."

The cost? It's expensive.

"You get what you pay for," according to Allen. "This model has so many safety nets and support systems, the teacher just has to take the first step as soon as a child first stumbles. But he or she can't wait. I take it a bit further and tell the teachers. 'You may not under any circumstances allow a child to fail in your room.'"

The Model

The program used in Jerry Allen's school is a school-wide reading reform model that was established in Baltimore in 1987. Now in 450 districts nationwide, the program serves children in districts ranging from some of the largest cities in the country to small rural villages. Just about all of these schools serve high-poverty students.

Like any school-wide reform model, this one requires broad support. Teachers are asked to put aside familiar methods and accept a new system. They receive three days of in-service training at the beginning of the school year, plus continuing in-service meetings.

The emphasis is on early intervention and prevention. A rigorous reading period lasts for one and one-half to two hours. Teachers at every grade level begin each session by reading a story aloud to children. The class then discusses the meaning, vocabulary, and structure of the story. In kindergarten and first grade, teachers focus on oral language and prereading skills. They ask students to retell and dramatize literature, as well as compose their own oral stories. The program also emphasizes phonemic awareness. In kindergarten or grade one, children begin with mini books, which they can read even if they know just a few letter sounds.

Children are grouped according to ability and disperse to their various levels during reading periods. Every eight weeks, they are reevaluated and, if it is warranted, moved along.

One major goal of the program is to keep children in the regular classroom and out of special education. Individual tutoring is key. Children who are falling behind the class receive 20-minute sessions with a teacher or tutor each day during times other than reading or math periods. The focus is the same material covered during the regular reading class. Other features include a bilingual curriculum, parent outreach, and a program facilitator at each school whose full-time job is to help the teachers to implement the model.

should be subsequently taught to extend their first language literary skills to reading in English.

Other language-minority children will arrive at school with no proficiency in English and speak a language for which the above conditions cannot be met—and for which there are insufficient numbers of children to justify the development of the local capacity to meet such conditions. In this case, the initial instructional priority should be developing the children's oral proficiency in English. Print materials may be used to support the development of English language skills. But formal reading instructions in English should be postponed until an adequate level of oral proficiency in English has been achieved. Ensuring this proficiency will require extremely rich and well-adapted oral language environments. In general, non-English speakers in the United States are highly motivated to learn English, but they still require an adequate amount of time and exposure to well-structured input from native speakers to do so.

"Parents need to understand that we are living in a society in which learning English and fostering the native language both are very important. We have parents in our system who may be only concerned with having their children learn English. But they do not understand that a lot of times it is done at the expense of their native language. Often the result is mediocre levels of achievement; many children will not learn how to read or write well solely in English because the language they think in, the language they function in, the language they speak at home is different.

Native language instruction has to be a part of the learning process. It's simply because, through native language instruction, children are able to communicate their needs, to acquire concepts, to express themselves, to ask questions, and to acquire English. English is the dominant language in America, but we live in a multicultural, multilingual world. There is tremendous benefit in being not only bilingual but also biliterate. In terms of children's futures—in high school, college, and the job market—having a second language is a great asset."

—Carmen DaCosta
Bilingual specialist
Early Childhood Programs
Chicago Public Schools

Children Unfamiliar with Standard English Dialect

Differences between the dialect children speak at home and the dialect taught at school may contribute to difficulties in learning to read. In the United States, some teachers, administrators, and policy makers view dialect differences not as regional variations, but as incorrect English. Some teachers develop low expectations for these students. Under these conditions, children are being placed at risk because of their unfamiliarity with standard English dialect.

As discussed in the previous two chapters, developing children's awareness of the sounds of words—their phonemic awareness—is a critical step toward helping them learn to read. However, what they need more specifically is an appreciation of the phonemes or sounds of words that are presumed in how the words are spelled. This is especially hard for dialect-speaking children. A teacher pointing out the "d" sound in the words "sold" or "find" can befuddle the African American child who pronounces these words "sol" and "fine." A child who pronounces the words "deaf" and "death" in the same way is likely to be confused if the teacher uses these words in a lesson on contrasting final consonants. However, these kinds of confusions in phonemic awareness and reading instruction can largely be avoided by making teachers more aware of dialect differences. A teacher who is sufficiently knowledgeable and sensitive about dialect will prepare materials and lessons that are consistent with the phonology, syntax, and vocabulary of the children's dialect.

Children Living in Communities in Poverty

Poverty undeniably poses numerous threats to children's educational prospects. Children in low-income families tend to have uneducated parents, lack adequate nutrition, live in poor communities, and attend substandard schools. All of these factors can be detrimental to reading.

However, all else being equal, coming from a low-income family, in and of itself, does not greatly increase a child's risk for learning to read, provided they are given the instruction and support they need. Therefore, poverty in individual families should not be used exclusively as an identifier for children at risk. It is more effective to identify children who come from families with low income status *and* attend a school with large numbers of poor students.

Schools with kindergartners who are poorly prepared in language and literacy skills must have programs that are better than or at least equivalent to the programs found in schools with well-prepared kindergartners. In order to provide such reading programs, schools with underprepared students need extra funding. To be effective, the extra funding should be used for methods with previously established success, and should be coupled with smaller student-teacher ratios, capable, experienced teachers and specialists, and a sufficient quantity of high-quality books and other materials.

What Can We Do Before Children Reach School?

"My biggest obstacle in teaching reading is the lack of experiences that some children are bringing to school—lack of language experiences involving reading, print, and concepts. Experiences like having your mother explain the types of fruit at the grocery store or playing with funnels in the bathtub. Experiences that come with having been talked to and read to."

—Emelie Parker
First grade teacher
Bailey's Elementary School
Fairfax County, Virginia

Health Care Professionals and Reading

Because of their regular contact with children during early childhood, pediatricians, and other health care and human service professionals have a responsibility to screen children for risk factors that could lead to reading difficulties. As early in the child's life as possible, health care professionals should identify problems, such as mental retardation, hearing impairment, early language impairment, and delays in expressive and receptive language milestones, as well as family histories of reading problems that could be passed on to children. In cases of hearing impairment, early identification and intervention is especially important and can make all the difference in whether or not a child becomes a successful reader.

Beyond routine screening, health care professionals have a wonderful opportunity to promote reading. At routine visits, they can help guide parents and encourage children's literacy development. In one program, volunteers in doctors' waiting rooms demonstrate for parents book-sharing and book-reading techniques, doctors prescribe parents to read books to their children, and books are given to parents with low incomes. Parents also receive information on the importance of reading and having books in the home. i

How Pediatricians and Health Care Professionals Can Help

At Regular and Other Checkups

- Model for parents how to talk to babies and children and respond to their attempts at language. Encourage them to do this.
- Encourage parents to play with language with their children, for example, reciting rhymes and singing songs.
- Encourage parents to make books, papers, and writing materials available and suggest that children should use reading and writing activities in daily play.
- Discuss with parents and children the importance of reading to and with children.
- Provide understandable brochures and videos in their waiting rooms (in the native languages of their patients) encouraging literacy-oriented activities with children.

"During the course of a day in a busy pediatrician's office, I don't think any of us does as well as we should. But promoting literacy should be a very big priority . . . . Every checkup should include some sort of developmental screening—even if informal, from observing how the child interacts with the parent in the room. If we can't get what we need that way, we should ask questions directly. After every visit, the pediatrician should assure himself or herself that the child is up to snuff developmentally. That's basic. . . . We have reading materials in every exam room—a bucket full of books to let families know that we believe reading is important. During checkups, I discuss literature with kids. I'll ask what they've been reading and tell them some of my favorite books from childhood. Sometimes I prescribe books for kids to read."

—Daniel Shapiro, M.D.
Pediatrician
Silver Spring, Maryland

Screening by Early Childhood Professionals 

Because they are one of the few professionals in contact with very young children, pediatricians, nurses, and other health care practitioners are in the best position to detect problems at routine checkups from infancy through preschool years. Day care and preschool settings also offer an important opportunity for early identification of the following kinds of risk:

Severe cognitive deficits

Within the normal range, IQ is moderately associated with future reading ability. But severe cognitive deficits are usually associated with very low, if any, reading achievement.

Hearing impairment

It has been well documented that children with hearing impairments are at risk of future reading difficulties. Although hard-of-hearing children tend to do better than deaf children, they are still at risk, even if they have good speaking abilities.

Early language impairment

Children acquire language at tremendously variable rates during the first four years of life. Yet some children are clearly behind by age two or three. This is an important signal. Delayed language development can be the first warning of a pervasive developmental disability, hearing impairment, or neurological problem. Any of these conditions puts a child at risk of future reading difficulties.

Often an evaluation by a speech-language professional reveals that these children have early language impairment. About 40 to 75 percent of preschoolers with such an impairment develop reading difficulties later—often along with other academic problems.

Expressive and receptive language delays

Children's development of language during preschool years is strongly related to how well they will later learn to read. An infant's achievement of "expressive" language milestones appears to have a particularly strong link to later reading achievement. Assessment of these milestones is part of regular well-baby visits and can be used to identify children at risk.

Children Whose Parents Have a History of Reading Difficulty
A child whose parents had trouble learning to read is not destined to failure. But such children face a substantially greater risk of reading problems. Once a child is having reading difficulties in school, pediatricians or educators often discover that someone else in the family has reading difficulties. It is wise for pediatricians to ask the parents of young children whether they had difficulty learning to read and, if so, to encourage them to lend extra enthusiasm to books and reading from the start—and to pay extra attention to signs of difficulty.

Developmental Interventions for the Youngest Children

"Many kids in our program have language delays. We really believe that, for them, exposure to language is key. Whether the problem is biological or environmental, you can go a long way toward increasing a child's learning ability and cognitive capacity. Giving an enriched environment and heavy exposure to language and language materials—this is effective early intervention and prevention."

—Jo Dennis
Director, therapeutic day care
Children's Institute International
Los Angeles, California

Most studies that examine the quality of preschools use broad-gauged tools that include language and literacy as only one small portion of the assessment. Such studies have found that it is precisely on measures of the language environment that preschool programs serving poor children scored in the inadequate range.

Strong language and literacy environments are especially effective for very young children who need an extra boost to promote their later success in reading. It is especially important for children who live in low-income communities and are slated to attend elementary schools with a poor track record in reading. Well-designed programs are also needed for individuals with specific difficulties, whether they are general cognitive ones, hearing impairments, or early language impairments. Children whose parents have a history of reading problems will also profit from well-designed language and literacy environments.

Catch Them from the Cradle: Earliest Interventions

Based on the tremendous influence of early childhood on later reading and academic success, it makes good sense to give children preventive early intervention if they appear headed for later reading problems or school failure. That is why federal and state governments give major funding to preschool programs nationwide. Unfortunately, researchers have often found disappointing results: education gains made in many preschool programs tend to dissipate as the children move through their elementary school years.

Many preschool programs are not as intensive as they could be. Children typically don't begin until age four, and then with only a half-day program. Other early childhood interventions have proven more successful by enrolling children earlier and providing more comprehensive services and curricula.

In one impressive program studied by researchers, children began attending in infancy (typically about four months old) and received a wide array of well-coordinated education, medical, and family outreach services. i The caregiver-to-child ratio was one-to-three, and so babies received a lot of direct individual attention from well-trained day care workers at the center. The center operated full days, year round. Daily activities for babies focused on cognitive and fine motor skills, social and self-help skills, language skills, and gross motor skills.

By the time children reached preschool level, the child-adult ratio gradually increased to one adult for every six children. Like any high-quality preschool, classrooms were equipped with centers for art, housekeeping, blocks, fine motor manipulatives, language, and literacy. In addition, caregivers and teachers were trained in language and literacy development. At age four, some children received training in phonological awareness in a 10-minute session, twice a week.

To help children make a successful transition into kindergarten, the program included a six-week summer transitional classroom experience in a large, socioeconomically mixed group similar to what they would encounter in public school.

The program also arranged for medical care on site at the child care center. Families received home visits for the purpose of parent education on child health and development, as well as parenting issues. Parents served on the center's advisory board and were invited to a series of educational workshops. Social events also brought families to the center.

Not surprisingly, the children's development was enhanced. From ages 18 to 54 months, they scored significantly higher on measures of intellectual development than the control group. At age five, they had higher IQs and better language skills. But what is most notable is that the positive impact was lasting. During a series of follow-up studies when children reached ages 8, 12, and 15, they were still outperforming the control groups on achievement tests. Significantly, fewer children had been held back a grade or placed in special education.

Time and again, research has confirmed that

* with early intervention, children with disabilities achieve developmental milestones more easily;

* with the right stimulation in early childhood, families and practitioners can help mitigate the lifelong effects of a child's disabling condition;

* among children from poor communities, early intervention can improve school achievement.

Reaching Out to Children's Homes

Because of the enormous influence of family on a child's school success, many family literacy interventions have arisen in recent years. These programs range vastly in intensity and type. But what most of them have in common is an effort to reach out to parents and caregivers with home visits from a parent educator, information on child development, and guidance on how to get children ready for kindergarten. In many family literacy programs, screening is available to determine if children have developmental delays.

Some family literacy programs reach out to parents even before their children are born, during the pregnancy. Other programs merely provide books to preschoolers, along with parent guidance on how to read effectively to children. Still other programs try to give parents themselves literacy training, as well as their children. Research on family literacy programs suggests that they have small but positive effects on school readiness, including small positive improvements in the reading materials available in children's homes, as well as improved parent expectations for their children's academic success.

Summary

It is important to note that, for children at risk of reading difficulties, high-quality experiences during preschool years cannot be seen as a way to prevent all reading difficulties. If a child has an enriched early childhood environment but attends a low-achieving elementary school with ineffective teaching, the child remains at risk. Indeed, the positive experiences of the early years will be muted if not followed by good instruction. Quality preschool followed up with high-quality primary education will reduce the number of cases of reading failure. There is, however, a small percentage of children who will have reading failure and for whom known interventions have not been successful.

Help in the Early Grades

To the extent that a child falls behind his or her peers in reading, that child is at risk of never reaching adequate literacy levels. i Any child who is falling behind should be able to get immediate and appropriate assistance. No assumptions about or labeling of the cause of the problem should be necessary. Unfortunately, under current funding systems, millions of children can get help only if they are classified as learning disabled or impaired in various ways.

If children are having difficulty in first grade reading achievement, their classrooms should be examined to see if they need improvement. If their classroom instruction is appropriate but they are having difficulty in reading achievement, they should immediately receive supplementary reading assistance with one-on-one tutoring by a well-qualified reading instructor. In order to be effective, tutoring sessions should be integrated with what the child is learning and doing in class.

The Need for Reading Specialists

Schools that lack or have abandoned reading specialist positions must reexamine their needs for specialists and provide the functional equivalent of such well-trained staff members. Reading specialists and other specialist roles need to be defined so that there is two-way communication between specialists and classroom teachers about the needs of all children at risk of and experiencing reading difficulties. Coordination is needed at the instructional level, so that children are taught with methodologies that are not fragmented. Schools that have reading specialists as well as special educators need to coordinate these roles. Schools need to ensure that all the specialists engaged in child study or individualized educational program (IEP) meetings for special education placement, early childhood intervention, out-of-classroom interventions, and classroom support are well informed about research in reading development and the prevention of reading difficulties.

The Community Is Needed

Much of this book has been devoted to parents, teachers, day care workers, tutors, and other professionals who work with children every day. Yet enormous power is also in the hands of school superintendents, managers, elected officials, and other policy makers—from the grassroots level to the national stage—who decide how our children are educated, where resources go, and which programs receive funding. If we are to succeed in ensuring that all children can read, then all parts of society must support and create the necessary conditions.

"Every adult professional in contact with parents and children—from pediatricians to retailers and even the business community—has the obligation to make children readers . . . . Children need to understand that reading can be anywhere. When you have five minutes of time, you can pick up a book, magazine, or whatever and read."

—Marilyn Hosea
National Head Start fellow and
Head Start administrator
Pasadena, California

Early Intervention in Reading

"We watch how they go about reading and writing, and where they need help," says Joetta Beaver, a reading teacher/leader in Arlington County Schools, Ohio. "You start with their strengths and then you move on to what they need to learn next."

One early intervention is for young readers who are having problems during their first year of reading instruction. The cornerstone of the program is extensive training for teachers, who then provide diagnostic, individualized one-on-one tutoring sessions each day.

Children from the lowest-performing fifth of the class are selected for the program. For 12 to 20 weeks, a specially trained teacher gives them a 30-minute lesson each day. These lessons consist of a variety of reading and writing activities, including reading familiar stories, reading a story that was read the day before, working with letters and/or words using magnetic letters, writing a story, assembling a cut-up story, and reading a new book that the child will read independently the next day.

This program has earned national recognition and praise for causing schools to recognize the value of providing extra help to children early in their school careers. Yet, the program has come under recent criticism for its relative neglect of phonics and high costs. Teacher training includes a year-long curriculum at a university training center and is followed by ongoing development in a professional network. The program is also costly because teachers spend about half of each day working one-to-one with only a few children. Although many tutoring programs use inexperienced volunteers, this program strives to give expert attention to the children who are struggling the most and often have complex needs.

"Most teachers get only one or two reading courses when they're in school," says Beaver. "Through the training, teachers get a better understanding of the reading process and how young children learn. Having a trained teacher makes all the difference in the world."

Volunteer Tutoring

"Three years ago, I went to the housing authority of our town and asked if I could organize people from my church to tutor children in a housing project. They said okay, so I started a program. Then I recruited eight other churches to get involved and start their own programs. All together we now serve about 350 kids a week in cooperation with their schools and teachers. We're not funded by any government program, but every student who comes has a single tutor. We pick the kids up in buses and bring them to our church at around 6 o'clock on Monday nights. About 80 adults show up to help. The kids have to sit down and work hard for at least 45 minutes with their tutors on their homework or reading. Then we feed them and play games in the gym. By 8 o'clock, they're back home."

"The most important thing about this is that the kids know that there are adults out there who care about them. Many of these kids don't get individualized attention except on tutoring night. These kids are all smart. It's just a matter of getting their own desire started. We've got so many kids who were getting D's and F's, but they were smart kids. After six months of tutoring program, they now get A's and B's."

—Jimmy England
Pharmacist and founder, church tutoring program
Jackson, Tennessee

How effective is volunteer tutoring?

How can it be used most effectively?

Good volunteer programs must include comprehensive screening procedures for selecting volunteers, professional training of tutors, and excellent supervision of their ongoing work with children. Volunteers are particularly helpful when they spend their time reading to children, giving children supported practice in oral reading, and allowing opportunities for enriching conversation. However, volunteers should not be used to provide primary or remedial instruction to children. Nor should they be expected to deal effectively with children who have serious reading problems. Volunteer tutors can provide very valuable practice and motivational support for children learning to read.

Reaching Out to Parents in High-Risk Neighborhoods

Children must have access to books if they are to read. But books in themselves are simply not enough. Children also need to have a caring adult to read to them and talk to them, preferably every day. In many high-risk families, parents may have poor reading skills themselves and not much experience with books. They may not know how to choose good literature or engage their children in reading. And they may not know how important daily reading is from infancy through early school years.

One unique effort located in Pennsylvania tries to get children and parents passionate about reading together. i In addition to distributing free high-quality books to thousands of low-income families, the program also sponsors Read-Aloud Parent Clubs. These groups meet weekly at libraries, schools, and public housing projects to help give parents helpful techniques and confidence for reading with their children. Over the course of 6 to 14 sessions, parents receive:

* a tour of the local public library and a library card,
* exposure to different types of books available for library borrowing,
* a free book at each session,
* tips for successful parent-child reading sessions,
* encouragement to read daily to children,
* an opportunity for club members to ask questions and discuss problems, and
* suggestions for other home literacy activities.

The parent book clubs were originally developed for Head Start parents, but since have expanded into public housing communities and for parents of Title I kindergartners. The program also includes a bookmobile—a library on wheels, which visits low-income communities and day care centers, encouraging children and adults to borrow books on a regular basis.

Tutoring Individual Children at Risk

In school lunchrooms, public housing projects, church basements, and libraries all across the nation, tutors spend time with children helping them learn to read. But what is the best way to go about this task? How can tutors be put to best use?

Two programs described below have had some significant successes in improving children's reading success. Both share a commitment to quality, with well-trained tutors, regular monitoring, and coordination with the child's school.

One program, based in Charlottesville, Virginia, provides one-to-one tutoring by community volunteers in a program that is designed to supplement instruction the child receives in class. i First and second grade children are recommended by their classroom teachers. Tutors are trained in research-based methods three times a year during two-hour sessions. At each school, a reading coordinator supervises 15 volunteer tutors and their tutees, and also provides ongoing training and support for the tutors. Two times a year, the coordinator assesses children individually to design an appropriate program, monitor progress, and coordinate with classroom teachers and parents.

The tutoring program consists of 45-minute sessions twice a week. During these sessions, students reread familiar storybooks, read new books, and practice writing. Word study is a unique aspect of the program and gives children practice with letter formation, sound segments within words, letter-sound correspondences, spelling patterns, and meanings. A quasi-experimental research design found significant improvements in alphabet recognition, speech to print abilities, phonemic awareness, word recognition, and reading accuracy of a first grade text.

A Texas-based program uses trained and paid paraprofessional tutors (college students, community residents, teacher aides) to deliver three to five weekly one-on-one tutoring sessions to low-performing readers throughout the school years. i Children in grades one to six are recommended by their teachers for the program.

Each child is assessed and placed into an ability level, ranging from those who are still learning their letters to those who are able to read at least the easiest books on their own. The curriculum combines explicit instruction on decoding skills with the use of small books that are ranked by difficulty level—including fiction and nonfiction—from emergent literacy level through fluency level. Sessions last for 45 minutes and always include reading and writing. Children are assessed every fifth session. One evaluation of this program shows that a set of sessions (taking about four to six months) typically raises a child's grade equivalent score by about a half year.

Conclusion

Children who do well in reading from the beginning rarely stumble later on. Those who have difficulty in the primary grades tend to remain behind their classmates as the years go by—even though they receive remediation. This fact, reconfirmed again and again, is a painful testimony to the importance of addressing reading difficulties as early as possible in a child's life. As important as it is to hold out hope for every struggling reader in our middle and high schools, there is no substitute for an all-out effort to ensure that all of our children start out right, so that they never have to experience the consequences of failure and frustration that are so prevalent in our schools.

"The way children initially are taught how to read is critical to their success. We've waited until children are struggling and then put so much money into remediation. But I'm just not sure how well that has worked. The way a child learns how to do something the first time makes all the difference."

—Jennifer Schindler,
Principal
El Vista Elementary School
Modesto, California

Glossary

Alphabetic Principle A writing system design principle that associates units from the limited set of phonemes of oral language with units from the limited set of letters of the alphabet, yielding a highly productive alphabetic writing system. Knowledge of the alphabetic principle is awareness that written words are composed of letters that are intentionally and conventionally related to phonemic segments of the words of oral language.

Big Books Oversized books that the offer opportunity to share the print and illustrations with a group of children in ways that one might share a standard sized book with just a few.

Comprehension Understanding: listening comprehension refers to spoken language, reading comprehension refers to written language.

Comprehensive Curricula Courses of study that include all the necessary content for achieving specific teaching and learning goals.

Curriculum Casualties Children whose reading difficulties arise from flaws in the design of regular classroom course of study, or its delivery.

Decoding Skills Skills in translating symbols (e.g., alphabet letters) into recognizable syllables and words.

Developmental Delay Delay, as measured by appropriate diagnostic instruments and procedures, in one or more of the areas of cognitive development, physical development, communication development, social or emotional development, and adaptive development.

Dialect A regional or social variety of a language distinguished by pronunciation, grammar, or vocabulary, especially a variety of speech differing from the standard literary language or speech pattern of the culture in which it exists. i

Early Language Impairment A failure to thrive in the development of one's native language; a significant and prolonged deviation from age related language milestones; a reduced capacity in expressive or receptive language or both. "Specific language impairment" is the preferred term if development thrives in cognitive, affective, and social spheres and is impaired only for language.

Emergent Literacy A range of activities and behaviors related to written language including those undertaken by very young children who depend on the cooperation of others and/or on creative play to deal with the material; reading and writing related activities and behaviors that change over time culminating in conventional literacy during middle childhood.

Emergent Reading Reading related activities and behaviors, especially those prior to a child's achieving the capacity to read fluently and conventionally; This includes (a) the attentive presence of a child while another reads for the child's benefit, (b) the execution of acts with materials related to reading, e.g., page turning, letter naming, and (c) the pretense of processing and/or comprehending written language.

Emergent Writing Writing related activities and behaviors, especially those prior to a child's achieving the capacity to write fluently and conventionally; includes (a) the attentive presence of a child while another writes according to the child's intentions, (b) the execution of acts with materials related to writing, e.g., scribbling letter-like forms, inventive spelling, and (c) the pretense of producing text to be read.

Expressive Language Capacity Accuracy, fluency, and appropriateness in producing language.

Fluency Achieving speed and accuracy in recognizing words and comprehending connected text, and coordinating the two.

Frustration Level/Reading Level at which a child's reading skills break down: fluency disappears, errors in word recognition are numerous, comprehension is faulty, recall is sketchy, and signs of emotional tension and discomfort become evident.

Intervention A supplementary program to address an identified or anticipated reading problem. Remedial interventions are aimed at school children who have been identified as achieving below expected levels. Preventive interventions are aimed at (younger) children who are thought to be at risk for developing reading problems.

Invented Spelling A child's spelling system based on letter names and/or sounds. It is also called inventive spelling, creative spelling, estimated spelling.

Language Milestones A significant point in language development, such as saying one's first word or beginning to combine words.

Literacy This includes reading, writing, and the creative and analytical acts involved in producing and comprehending texts.

Morphology The aspects of language structure related to the ways words are formed from prefixes, roots and suffixes (e.g., "mis-spell-ing") and are related to each other.

Onset The consonant(s) at the start of a syllable; the remainder of the syllable is called its "rime." In "swift," "sw" is the onset and "ift" is the rime.

Orthographic Awareness Knowing that letters and diacritics represent the spoken language; attending to predictable and frequent spelling patterns. (A diacritic is a mark, such as the cedilla of façade or the acute accents of résumé, added to a letter to indicate a special phonetic value or distinguish words that are otherwise graphically identical.) i

Orthography A method of representing spoken language by letters and diacritical marks, spelling.

Phonemes In oral language, the small units that combine to form syllables and words (e.g., the phonemes in the standard English words "bit" and "hit" are the same except for the first segment and the word "hint" has one more phoneme that the word "hit.").

Phoneme Segmentation To break words into phonemes.

Phonemic Awareness A special kind of "phonological awareness" (defined below) involving the smallest units of oral language, phonemes.

Phonics Instructional practices that emphasize how spellings are related to speech sounds in systematic ways; letter-sound correspondences.

Phonological Awareness Knowing that oral language has structure that is separate from meaning; attending to the sub-lexical structure (i.e., structure within words) of oral language, e.g., "beg" has one syllable and three phonemes, "egg" has one syllable and two phonemes.

Phonology The aspects of language structure related to the distinctive features for the representation, production, and reception of sounds of language.

Readiness To be prepared for instruction.

Reading Problem Low achievement in reading or some key component of reading.

Receptive Language Capacity Accuracy, fluency, and appropriateness in understanding language.

Reciprocal Teaching A teaching process in which teachers and students take turns asking and answering questions in order to comprehend text and to learn comprehension strategies.

Rime The portion of a syllable that follows the "onset" (see above).

Risk Factor A characteristic of a child or of the child's home, family, or community, such that variation in that characteristic is associated with variation in reading achievement. (These correlations need not be causal, just informative about the early identification of children at risk.)

Speech Discrimination Accurate identification of the distinctions in the range and characteristics of sounds used in oral languages.

Syllable A unit of spoken language. In English, a syllable can consist of a vowel sound alone or a vowel sound with one or more consonant sounds preceding and following.

Syntax The aspects of language structure related to the ways in which words are put together to form phrases, clauses, and sentences.

Word Attack An aspect of reading instruction that includes intentional strategies for learning to decode, sight read, and recognize written words.

Word Decoding An aspect of reading that involves deriving a pronunciation for a printed sequence of letters based on knowledge of spelling-sound correspondences.

Word Recognition In reading, identifying as known words those that have been decoded or processed as whole words and associating the known words with their meaning and use in language being read.

For More Information

Page Number	Source
2	The content of this book is based on a study by a committee of some of the nation's most eminent researchers, who were appointed by the National Research Council of the National Academy of Sciences and the National Academy of Engineering to review current scientific research in the field of early reading development. The work of the Committee on the Prevention of Reading Difficulties in Young Children resulted in the publication of *Preventing Reading Difficulties in Young Children* (National Academy Press, 1998), which includes its complete scientific assessment and recommendations.

The focus of that report is prevention. In it we tried to sketch the conditions under which reading is likely to develop most easily—conditions that include stimulating preschool environments, excellent reading instruction, and the absence of a wide array of risk factors. In fact, many children from poor and uneducated families learn to read well, even without excellent preschool classroom experiences or superb early reading instruction. Nonetheless, with an eye to reducing risk and preventing failure, we focused on ways to provide the best possible situation for every child.

Two additional documents developed by educational organizations might be of interest to the readers of this book.

- Learning First Alliance. (1998). *Every Child Reading: An Action Plan.* (Learning First Alliance member organizations are American Association of Colleges for Teacher Education, American Association of School Administrators, American Federation of Teachers, Association for Supervision and Curriculum Development, Council of Chief State School Officers, Education Commission of the States, National Association of Elementary School Principals, National Association of Secondary School Principals, National Association of State Boards of Education, National Education Association, National Parent Teacher Association, and National School Boards Association.) 1001 Connecticut Ave., NW, Suite 335, Washington, DC, 202/296-5220.
- International Reading Association and the National Association for the Education of Young Children. (1998). Learning to read and write: developmentally appropriate practices for young children. *Young Children* 53:30-46.

19 We found several sources helpful in developing these activities

- Lynn, L. (1997). Helping children develop oral-language skills: 10 activities teachers and parents can do. *The Harvard Education Letter* 13(4).
- Whitehurst, G.J., F.L. Falco, C.J. Lonigan, J.E. Fischel, B.D. DeBaryshe, M., C. Valdez-Menchaca, and M. Caulfield. (1988). Accelerating language development through picture book reading. *Developmental Psychology* 24:552-559.
- *Helping Your Baby Learn to Talk.* (1995). U.S. Department of Education, Office of Educational Research and Improvement, National Institute on Early Childhood Development and Education.
- *Ready*Set*Read for Families.* (1997). U.S. Department of Education, America Reads Challenge.

20 *Green Eggs and Ham* by Dr. Seuss. (1960). New York: Random House.

21 *Friends Old and New: Picture Songbook* by Linda Swears. (1994). Greensboro, NC: Kindermusik International, Inc.

22 Dr. Seuss wrote and illustrated 42 books, published by Random House. They are listed below.

- And to Think That I Saw It on Mulberry Street
- The 500 Hats of Bartholomew Cubbins

- The King's Stilts
- Horton Hatches the Egg
- McElligot's Pool
- Thidwick the Big-Hearted Moose
- Bartholomew and the Oobleck
- If I Ran the Zoo
- Scrambled Eggs Super!
- Horton Hears a Who!
- On Beyond Zebra!
- If I Ran the Circus
- How the Grinch Stole Christmas!
- Yertle the Turtle and Other Stories
- Happy Birthday to You!
- The Sneetches and Other Stories
- Dr. Seuss's Sleep Book
- I Had Trouble in Getting to Solla Sollew
- The Cat in the Hat Songbook
- I Can Lick 30 Tigers Today! And Other Stories
- I Can Draw It Myself
- The Lorax
- Did I Ever Tell You How Lucky You Are?
- Hunches and Bunches
- The Butter Battle Book
- Oh, the Places You'll Go!
- The Cat in the Hat
- The Cat in the Hat Comes Back
- One Fish Two Fish Red Fish Blue Fish
- Green Eggs and Ham
- Hop on Pop
- Dr. Seuss's ABC
- Fox in Socks
- The Foot Book
- Mr. Brown Can Moo! Can You?
- Marvin K. Mooney Will You Please Go Now!
- The Shape of Me and Other Stuff
- There's a Wocket in My Pocket!
- Oh, the Thinks You Can Think!
- The Cat's Quizzer
- I Can Read with My Eyes Shut!
- Oh Say Can You Say?

22 Haines, B.J. and L.L. Gerber. (1995). *Leading Young Children to Music.* Fifth Edition. Upper Saddle River: Merrill/Prentice-Hall. Reprinted by permission.

22 Raffi recorded this song on a videotape titled "Raffi in Concert with the Rise and Shine Band." (1988). A&M video, PO Box 118, Hollywood, Calif 90028.

26 *Every Grownup Is a Famous Storyteller.* (1997). The Connecticut Commission on Children, 18-20 Trinity Street, Hartford, CT 06106. 860/240-0290

28 *Ready*Set*Read for Families.* (1997). U.S. Department of Education, America Reads Challenge.

29 High-quality children's magazines also serve as a rich source of print material. A few examples are listed

- *Turtle Magazine for Preschool Kids,* P.O. Box 420235, Palm Coast, FL 32142. 904/447-0818
- *Ladybug,* The Cricket Magazine Group, Box 7434, Red Oak, IA 51591-2434. 800/827-0227
- *Click,* Box 7499, Red Oak, IA 51591-2499. 800/827-0227

32, 33 Clay, M. (1975). *What Did I Write?* Portsmouth, NH: Heinemann Educational Books.

34 *Helping Your Child Learn to Read.* (1993). U.S. Department of Education, Office of Educational Research and Improvement.

35 Many companies produce cassette tapes to accompany children's books. A few examples are listed.

- *Goodnight Moon* by Margaret Wise Brown. Available from Harper Collins Publishers, Inc., 10 East 53rd Street, New York, NY 10022.
- *Kinderkittens Show-and-Tell* by Stephanie Calmenson. Available from Scholastics Cassettes, Scholastic, Inc., 555 Broadway, New York, NY 10012.
- *The Frog Prince* narrated by Robert Guillaume. Available from the Confetti Entertainment Company, Inc., P.O. Box 1155, Studio City, CA 91614.

• *Lyle, Lyle Crocodile* by Bernard Waber. Available from Houghton Mifflin Co., 222 Berkeley Street, Boston, MA 02116.
• *Grover and the Package* by Michaela Muntean. Available from Golden Books, Western Publishing Company, Inc., Racine, WI 53404.
• *Arthur Meets the President* by Marc Brown. Available from Little Brown & Co., 1271 Avenue of the Americas, New York, NY 10020.

36 Munsch, R.N. and M. Martchenko. (1980). *The Paper Bag Princess.* Toronto: Annick Press.

45 • Hohmann, M. and D. Weikert. (1995). *Educating Young Children.* Ypsilanti, MI: High/Scope Press.

Also see Schweinhart, L.J., et al.
• (1985). Effects of the Perry Preschool Program on youths through age 19: A summary. *Topics in Early Childhood Special Education Quarterly* 5(2): 26-35.
• (1986). Consequences of three preschool curriculum models through age 15. *Early Childhood Research Quarterly* 1(1):15-45.

46 *Ready*Set*Read for Caregivers.* (1997). U.S. Department of Education, America Reads Challenge.

46 • Adams, M.J., B.R. Foorman, I. Lundberg, and T.D. Beeler. (1998). *Phonemic Awareness in Young Children.* Baltimore: Paul H. Brookes Pub. Co. 800/638-3775
• Byrne, B. and R. Fielding-Barnsley. (1989). Phonemic awareness and letter knowledge in the child's acquisition of the alphabetic principle. *Journal of Educational Psychology* 81:313-321.
• Byrne, B. and R. Fielding-Barnsley. (1993). Evaluation of a program to teach phonemic awareness to young children: A 1-year follow-up. *Journal of Educational Psychology* 85:104-111.

47 *Friends Old and New: Picture Songbook* by Linda Swears. (1994). Greensboro, NC: Kindermusik International, Inc.

48 *The Eentsy, Weentsy Spider: Fingerplays and Other Action Rhymes* by Joanna Cole and Stephanie Calmeson. (1991). New York: Mulberry Press.

48 • Adams, M.J., B. R. Foorman, I. Lundberg, and T. D. Beeler. (1998).

Phonemic Awareness in Young Children. Baltimore: Paul H. Brookes Pub. Co. 800/638-3775

- *Helping Your Child Learn to Read.* (1993). U.S. Department of Education, Office of Educational Research and Improvement.

This poem, The Spider, is written by Frank Collymore and published in

- Agard, J. and G. Nichols (Editors) and C. Felstead (Illustrator). (1990). *A Caribbean Dozen: Poems from Caribbean Poets.* Cambridge, MA: Candlewick Press.

Additional examples of books of poetry for young children include

- Prelutsky, J. (Selector) and M. Bown (Illustrator). (1986). *Read-Aloud Rhymes for the Very Young.* New York: Alfred A. Knopf.
- Slier, D. (Editor) and C. Van Wright and Y. Hu (Illustrators). (1991). *Make a Joyful Sound: Poems for Children by African-American Poets.* New York: Checkerboard Press.

49 McGee, L.M. and D.J. Richgels. (1990). *Literacy's Beginnings: Supporting Young Readers and Writers.* Needham Heights, MA: Allyn and Bacon.

51
- Lynn, L. (1997). Helping children develop oral-language skills: 10 activities teachers and parents can do. *The Harvard Education Letter* 13(4).
- *Helping Your Child Learn to Read.* (1993). U.S. Department of Education, Office of Educational Research and Improvement.

51 Paley, V.G. (1986). *Mollie Is Three: Growing Up in School.* Chicago: University of Chicago Press.

52 *Stony Brook Reading & Language*
- Grover J. (Russ) Whitehurst, Ph.D. Professor of Psychology and Pediatrics, State University of New York at Stony Brook, Stony Brook, NY 11794-2500. website: www.whitehurst.sbs.sunysb.edu
- Whitehurst, G.J., F.L. Falco, C.J. Lonigan, J.E. Fischel, B.D. DeBaryshe, M.C. Valdez-Menchaca, and M. Caulfield. (1988). Accelerating language development through picture book reading. *Developmental Psychology* 24:552-559.

52 Kasza, K. (1992). *A Mother for Choco.* New York: G.P. Putnam's Sons.

53 *Getting Books in Children's Hands: The Great Book Flood of 1996.* Susan Neuman, Ph.D., Associate Professor, Temple University, Ritter Hall (003-00), Philadelphia, PA 19122.

54 Adams, M. (1994). *Beginning to Read.* Cambridge, MA: M.I.T. Press.

56 Paley, V.G. (1986). *Mollie Is Three: Growing Up in School.* Chicago: University of Chicago Press.

57 Hohmann, C., B. Carmody, and C. McCabe-Branz. (1995). *High/Scope Buyer's Guide to Children's Software.* Ypsilanti, MI: High/Scope Press.

57 *Reader Rabbit's Ready for Letters.* The Learning Company, 6493 Kaiser Dr., Fremont, CA 94555. 800/852-2255

57 *Kid Pix.* Broderbund Software, PO Box 61215, 500 Redwood Blvd., Novato, CA 94948-6121. 800/521-6263

57 *Living Books.* Random House/Broderbund Co., P.O. Box 6144 Novato, CA 94948-6144. 800/ 776-4724

57 *A to Zap.* Sunburst Communications, 101 Castleton St., Pleasantville, NY 10570. 800/321-7511

57 *Bailey's Book House.* Edmark Corporation, PO Box 3218, Redmond, WA 98073-3218. 800/426-0856

57 *The Playroom.* Broderbund Software, PO Box 61215, 500 Redwood Blvd., Novato, CA 94948-6121. 800/521-6263

66 The reading series in your child's school most likely includes many activities in this area. In addition, there are a number of books with similar activities. Examples of these are

- Fountas, I.C., and G.S. Pinnell. (1995). *Guided Reading: Good First Teaching for All Children.* Portsmouth, NH: Heinemann Educational Books.
- Bear, D.R., M. Invernizzi, S. Templeton, and F. Johnston. (1996). *Words Their Way.* Columbus, Ohio: Merrill.

Parents might also be interested in activities published in documents such as

- *You Can Help Your Child with Reading and Writing.* (1994). Edinfo Press, P.O. Box 5247, Bloomington, IN 47407. 800/925-7853
- *Helping Your Child Learn to Read.* (1993). U.S. Department of Education, Office of Educational Research and Improvement.
- *Read*Right*Now.* (1997) U.S. Department of Education, America Reads Challenge.

66 • Adams, M.J., B.R. Foorman, I. Lundberg, and T.D. Beeler. (1998). *Phonemic Awareness in Young Children.* Baltimore: Paul H. Brookes Pub. Co. 800/638-3775

- Griffith, P.L. and M.W. Olson. (1992). Phonemic awareness helps beginning readers break the code. *The Reading Teacher* 45:516-523.
- Yopp, H.P. (1995). Read-Aloud Books for Developing Phonemic Awareness: An Annotated Bibliography. *Reading-Teacher* 48:538-542.
- Yopp, H.P. (1992). Developing Phonemic Awareness in Young Children. *Reading-Teacher* 45:696-703.

70 Paley, V.G. (1981). *Wally's Stories: Conversations in the Kindergarten.* Cambridge, MA: Harvard University Press.

74 A 1992 recording of Ella Jenkins called "Come Dance by the Ocean" and a 1989 recording of Ella Jenkins called "You'll Sing a Song and I'll Sing a Song" include many of these features. They are available from Rounder Records, One Camp Street, Cambridge, MA 02140.

78 The reading series in your child's school most likely includes many activities in this area. In addition, there are a number of books with similar activities. Examples of these are

- Fountas, I.C. and G.S. Pinnell. (1995). *Guided Reading: Good First Teaching for All Children.* Portsmouth, NH: Heinemann Educational Books.
- Bear, D.R., M. Invernizzi, S. Templeton, and F. Johnston. (1996). *Words Their Way.* Columbus, Ohio: Merrill.

Parents might also be interested in documents such as

- *Evaluating Commercial Phonics Packages.* The International Reading Association, 800 Barksdale Road, P.O. Box 8139, Newark, DE 19714-8139.

- *Read*Right*Now.* (1997). U.S. Department of Education, America Reads Challenge.

82 The reading series in your child's school most likely includes many activities in this area. In addition, there are a number of books with similar activities. Examples of these are

- Adams, M.J., B.R. Foorman, I. Lundberg, and T.D. Beeler. (1998). *Phonemic Awareness in Young Children.* Baltimore: Paul H. Brookes Pub. Co. 800/638-3775
- Bear, D.R., M. Invernizzi, S. Templeton, and F. Johnston. (1996). *Words Their Way.* Columbus, Ohio: Merrill.

90 The reading series in your child's school most likely includes many activities in this area. In addition, there are a number of books with similar activities. Examples of these are

- Fountas, I.C. and G.S. Pinnell. (1995). *Guided Reading: Good First Teaching for All Children.* Portsmouth, NH: Heinemann Educational Books.
- Bear, D.R., M. Invernizzi, S. Templeton, and F. Johnston. (1996). *Words Their Way.* Columbus, Ohio: Merrill.

96 *Four Blocks.* Patricia Cunningham and Dorothy Hall, Box 7266 WFU, Winston Salem, NC 27109.

96 The reading series in your child's school most likely includes many activities in this area. In addition, there are a number of books with similar activities. Examples of these are

- Fountas, I.C. and G.S. Pinnell. (1995). *Guided Reading: Good First Teaching for All Children.* Portsmouth, NH: Heinemann Educational Books.
- Beck, I., M.G. McKeown, and R.L. Hamilton. (1997). *Questioning the Author: An Approach for Enhancing Student Engagement With Text.* Newark, NJ: International Reading Association.

Parents might also be interested in children's magazines which provide a great resource. Some examples include

- *Jack and Jill,* P.O. Box 420235, Palm Coast, FL 32142. 904/447-0818

- *Spider,* The Cricket Magazine Group, Box 7434, Red Oak, IA 51591-2434. 800/827-0227
- *Muse,* Box 7468, Red Oak, IA 51591-2499. 800/827-0227

99 Hot Cross Buns
Just in case you wanted a complete recipe, here it is.

This is basic but tasty.

2 pkgs active dry yeast
1/3 c water
1/3 c milk, scalded
1/2 c salad oil
1/3 c sugar
3/4 tsp salt
3 1/2 to 4 c sifted flour
1/2 to 1 tsp cinnamon
3 beaten eggs
2/3 c currants
1 slightly beaten egg white
sifted confectioners' sugar

Soften yeast in warm water. Combine milk, oil, sugar, and salt; cool to lukewarm. Sift together 1 c flour and the cinnamon; stir into milk mixture. Add eggs; beat well. Stir in softened yeast and currants. Add remaining flour (or a little more or less to make a soft dough). Cover with damp cloth; and let rise in warm place till double (about 1 1/2 hr). Punch down.

Roll or pat out to 1/2 inch on lightly floured surface. Cut in rounds with 2 1/2 inch biscuit cutter; shape in buns. Place on greased baking sheet about 1 1/2 inches apart. Cover and let rise in warm place until almost double (about 1 hr). If desired, cut shallow cross in each bun with sharp scissors or knife. Brush tops with egg white. Bake at 375° about 12 minutes or until done. Add confectioners' sugar (about 3/4 c) to the remaining egg white. Use this as a frosting for piping crosses on warm buns.

Makes about 2 dozen.

103 *Helping Your Child Learn to Read.* (1993). U.S. Department of Education, Office of Educational Research and Improvement.

106 Staton, J., R.W. Shuy, J.K. Peyton, and L. Reed. (1998). *Dialogue Journal Interaction: Classroom, Linguistic, Social, and Cognitive Views.* Norwood, NJ: Ablex.

110 Stahl, S.A., K. Heubach, and C.E. Davus. (1997.) *Fluency-Oriented Reading Instruction*. Reading research report No. 79. Athens, GA: National Reading Research Center.

111 Pressley, M., J. Rankin, and L. Yokoi. (1996). A survey of instructional practices of outstanding primary-level literacy teachers. *Elementary School Journal* 93:363-384.

112
- Palincsar, A.S. and A.L. Brown. (1984). Reciprocal teaching of comprehension-fostering and comprehension-monitoring activities. *Cognition and Instruction* 1:117-175.
- Palincsar, A.S., A.L. Brown, and J.C. Campione. (1993). First-grade dialogues for knowledge acquisition and use. In E. Forman, N. Minick, and C.A. Stone (Eds.), *Contexts for Learning: Sociocultural Dynamics in Children's Development*. New York: Oxford University Press.

120 Breakthrough to Literacy. 131 Technology Innovation Center, Oakdale, IA 52319. 800/874-2851

120 Waterford Early Reading Program. 1590 East 9400 South, Sandy, UT 84093. 801/576-4900

120 Little Planet Publishing. P.O. Box 158427, Nashville, TN 37215-8427. 800/947-2248

121 Hohmann, C., B. Carmody, and C. McCabe-Branz. (1995). *High/Scope Buyer's Guide to Children's Software*. Ypsilanti, MI: High/Scope Press.

121 *The Treehouse*. Broderbund Software, PO Box 61215, 500 Redwood Blvd., Novato, CA 94948-6121. 800/521-6263

121 *Reader Rabbit 2*. The Learning Company, 6493 Kaiser Dr., Fremont, CA 94555. 800/852-2255

121 *My Own Stories*. MECC Minnesota Ed Computing Corp., 6160 Summit Dr., Minneapolis, MN 55430-4003. 800/685-6322

129 *Collections for Young Scholars*. Open Court Publishing Company of SRA/McGraw-Hill, New York.

131 *Success for All.* Robert Slavin, CRESPAR, 3505 North Charles St., Baltimore, MD 21218-2498. 410/516-8800

134 *Reach Out and Read (ROAR).* Boston City Hospital, Mat 5, 818 Harrison Avenue, Boston, MA 02118. 617/534-5701

136 In addition, your local school system can provide information and contacts regarding early identification, screening, and assessment services that are part of the Individuals with Disabilities Education Act.

138

- Campbell, F.A., and C.T. Ramey. (1994). Effects of early intervention on intellectual and academic achievement: A follow up study of children from low income families. *Child Development* 65:684-698.
- Campbell, F.A., and C.T. Ramey. (1993). Mid-Adolescent Outcomes for High-Risk Students: An Examination of the Continuing Effects of Early Intervention. ERIC document ED358919.

140 *Learning to Read, Reading to Learn: Helping Children with Learning Disabilities to Succeed.* U.S. Department of Education, Office of Special Education Programs. 202/205-5465

141 *Reading Recovery.* Gay Su Pinnell or Carol Lyons, The Ohio State University, Ramseyer 200, 29 W. Woodruff, Columbus, Ohio 43210.

143 *Beginning with Books.* Elizabeth Segel, Ph.D., Co-Director, Beginning with Books, 7101 Hamilton Ave., Pittsburgh PA 15208. segele@clpgh.org

144 *Book Buddies.* Connie Juel, Director of Studies in Learning to Read, University of Virginia, 405 Emmet St., Charlottesville, VA. 804/924-1380

144 *Reading One-One.* Professor George Farkas, University of Texas at Dallas. farkas@utdallas.edu

148,149 *American Heritage Dictionary of the English Language:* Third Edition, (1994). Boston: Houghton Mifflin Company.

Internet Resources

There are many Internet sites where you can find even more resources, for example,

READING/LITERACY

America Reads Challenge
Calls on Americans to support teachers to ensure that every American child can read well and independently by the end of 3rd grade.
http://www.ed.gov/inits/americareads/

International Reading Association
Association home page with resources on improving the quality of reading instruction.
http://www.reading.org/

National Center for Literacy
Information on literacy and many useful links.
http://www.nifl.gov

National Institute of Child Health and Human Development
Includes information on reading initiatives in this branch of the federal government.
http://www.nih.gov/nichd/html/about_nichd.html

Reading Is Fundamental
Provides tips for parents and volunteers.
http://www.si.edu/rif

CHILDREN'S LITERATURE

American Library Association
More than 100 libraries register for America Links Up campaign.
http://www.ala.org

The Internet Public Library Youth Division
Lots of fun and educational stuff for children to see and do.
http://www.ipl.org/youth/

LITERACY RELATED TELEVISION

Children's Television Workshop
Provides parents with school and literacy related information.
http://www.ctw.org

Public Broadcasting Service
A children's home page with PBS children's shows characters.
http://www.pbs.org/kids/

CHILDREN WITH DISABILITIES

SERI Parents & Educator's Resources
A site with links to resources for parents and teachers.
http://www.hood.edu/seri/parents.htm

National Information Center for Children and Youth with Disabilities
NICHCY is the national information and referral center that provides information on disabilities and disability-related issues for families, educators, and other professionals.
http://www.nichcy.org/#about

Parents Helping Parents
Parent organization with information on disabilities.
http://www.php.com/

Family Village
Web site with many resources on disabilities.
http://www.familyvillage.wisc.edu/

IDEA The Law
A site with links to resources for parents and teacher about the Individuals with Disabilities Education Act.
http://ed.gov/offices/OSERS/IDEA/the_law.html

Office of Special Education Programs
A site with links to resources for parents and teacher, including a link to "Learning to Read/Reading to Learn."
http://www.ed.gov/offices/OSERS/OSEP/index.html

HOME AND SCHOOL

Partnership for Family Involvement
The mission of this group is to promote children's learning through the development of family-school-community partnerships.
http://www.ed.gov/PFIE

PARENTING

Parent Soup
Web site with many resources on parenting.
http://www.parentsoup.com/

The Parent's Place
Web site with many resources on parenting.
http://www.parentsplace.com/

CHILD HEALTH

Dr. Green's House Calls
Site with information on specific medical questions concerning children.
http://www.drgreene.com/

Kids' Health
Site on children's health with a section for parents on specific medical questions.
http://kidshealth.org/

Acknowledgments

Many people contributed in many different ways to the completion of this book, and we are most grateful for their efforts. First, the committee and staff would like to acknowledge Ellen Schiller (U.S. Department of Education), Naomi Karp (U.S. Department of Education), and Reid Lyon (National Institutes of Health) for assistance given during the project. Louis Danielson, Tom Hehir, Judith Heumann, Kent McGuire, and Marshal Smith of the U.S. Department of Education and Duane Alexander of the National Institutes of Health provided support and encouragement. Our thanks to Rebecca Fitch (U.S. Department of Education) and Frederick Mosher (Carnegie Corporation of New York) for their help in developing plans for liaison activities.

During the information-gathering phase of our work, a number of people made presentations and gave advice to the committee: Elizabeth Segal (Beginning with Books); Marcia Invernizzi (Book Buddies); Andrew Hayes (Comprehensive Family Literacy Program); John Guthrie (Concept Oriented Reading Instruction); Bob Stark (Early ID: Reading Early Identification and Intervention); Barbara Taylor (Early Intervention in Reading); Jerry Zimmerman (Foundations in Reading); Sabra Gelfond (Fast ForWord); Annette Dove and Pia Rebello (Home Instruction Program for Preschool Youngsters-HIPPY); Darcy Vogel (Intergenerational Tutoring Program); Ethna Reid (Keyboarding, Reading, Spelling); Bob Lemire and Kathy Hook (Phonics Based Reading); George Farkas (Reading One-One); M. Trika Smith-Burke (Reading Recovery); James Wendorf, Linda Gambrell, and Suzanne Kealey (RIF's Running Start Program); John Nunnary (Success For All); Marilyn Howard (Auditory Discrimination in Depth). We are grateful for their valuable contributions.

There are a number of additional people who gave advice specific to this book; our thanks to Valorie Burgess (Children's Learning Center, MD), Anne Colgate (Children's Learning Center, MD), Carmen DaCosta (Chicago Public Schools, IL), Jo Dennis (Children's Institute International, CA), Susan Derber (Springfield Public

Schools, IL), Jimmy England (Church Tutoring Program, TN), Ethelyn Hamilton-Frezel (New Orleans Public Schools, LA), Scott Hirose (Queens Child Guidance Center, NY), Marilyn Hosea (Head Start, CA), Emelie Parker (Fairfax County Public Schools, VA), Jennifer Schindler (Modesto Public Schools, CA), Daniel Shapiro (Pediatrician, MD), and Grover Whitehurst (Stony Brook Reading and Language, NY).

This book has been reviewed by individuals chosen for their diverse perspectives and technical expertise, in accordance with procedures approved by the National Research Council's Report Review Committee. The purpose of this independent review is to provide candid and critical comments that will assist the authors and the National Research Council in making the published book as sound as possible and to ensure that the book meets institutional standards for objectivity, evidence, and responsiveness to the study charge.

We also wish to thank the following individuals for their participation in the official review of this book: Carol Copple (National Association for the Education of Young Children, Washington, D.C.), Margaret Heritage (Seeds University Elementary School, University of California at Los Angeles), Peggy Kaye (education consultant, New York, New York), Frederick Mosher (Carnegie Corporation, New York, New York), P. David Pearson (College of Education, Michigan State University), Richard Wagner (Department of Psychology, Florida State University). While the individuals listed above have provided many constructive comments and suggestions, responsibility for the final content of this book rests solely with the authoring committee and the National Research Council.

Throughout the research, conceptualization, and writing phases of this work, our coeditor, Peg Griffin, was an invaluable colleague—a strong-minded collaborator, a tireless writer, and a reliably good-natured colleague. Laura Schenone provided the foundation for the book, taking the information from our main report and developing text and formats to make the document interesting to a wide audience. Three committee members, Marilyn Adams, Hollis Scarborough, and Elizabeth Sulzby, provided extra assistance with this book; the final product was enhanced greatly by their attention, as well as from the editorial attention of Christine McShane. Alexandra Wigdor, director of the Division on Education, Labor, and Human Performance, provided guidance and support throughout the project. Sharon Vandivere ably assisted the committee in their work. At the National Academy Press, many have collaborated to turn the committee's work into a visual reality. We are especially grateful to Francesca Moghari for her graphic design, which has added both beauty and meaning to the original manuscript. Thanks also to Sally Stanfield for keeping the project on track and to Sally Groom for illustrating the reading pillar with such charm. The committee extends its sincere thanks and appreciation to all those who assisted us in our work.

Catherine Snow, *Chair*
Susan Burns, *Study Director*
Committee on the Prevention of Reading
Difficulties in Young Children

Credits

Page i, © Jeffry W. Myers/Stock, Boston; **page iii**, © Lambert/Archive Photo; **page iv** (from top), © Amy Etra/PhotoEdit; © Jeffry W. Myers/Stock, Boston; National Research Council (NRC) family photo archives; Patton Photographer; Patton Photographer; Photodisk; **page v** (from top), Paul Hartmann, Photography; Paul Hartmann, Photography; Photodisk; Paul Hartmann, Photography; Paul Hartmann, Photography; **page vi**, Foreword TK; **page viii**, Photodisk; **page 1**, © Amy Etra/PhotoEdit; **page 2**, NRC family photo archives; **page 3**, Paul Hartmann, Photography; **page 5**, Paul Hartmann, Photography; **page 6**, NRC family photo archives; **page 7**, drawing by Sally Groom; **page 8**, NRC family photo archives; **page 9**, Photodisk; **page 11**, Paul Hartmann, Photography; **page 12**, Paul Hartmann, Photography; **page 13**, Patton Photographer; **page 14**, Patton Photographer; **page 15**, Photodisk; **page 16**, © Tony Freeman/PhotoEdit; **page 18**, Photodisk; **page 20**, NRC family photo archives; **page 21**, "Teddy Bear," © 1994, edited by Sandra Reichenbach. Kindermusik ® International, Inc., reprinted by permission; **page 22**, "Ba-Be-Bi-Bo-Bu,"reprinted by permission of B. Joan E. Haines, from Haines, B.J. and L.L. Gerber. (1995). *Leading Young Children to Music.* Fifth Edition. Upper Saddle River: Merrill/Prentice-Hall; **page 23**, Patton Photographer; **page 24**, NRC family photo archives; **page 26**, NRC family photo archives; **page 28**, Photodisk; **page 29**, NRC family photo archives; **page 31**, Photodisk; **page 33**, © Jeffry W. Myers/Stock, Boston; **page 35**, NRC family photo archives; **page 36**, Patton Photographer; **page 37**, NRC family photo archives; **page 38**, NRC family photo archives; **page 39**, NRC family photo archives; **page 40**, NRC family photo archives; **page 41**, NRC family photo archives; **page 42**, Paul Hartmann, Photography; **page 43**, © Joseph Schuyler/Stock, Boston; **page 44**, Patton Photographer; **page 45**, NRC family photo archives; **page 47**, "I Can Hear the Rain," © 1994, edited by Sandra Reichenbach. Kindermusik ® International, Inc., reprinted by permission; **page 49**, Patton Photographer; **page 50**, NRC family photo archives; **page 51**, Patton Photographer; **page 53**, Paul Hartmann, Photography; **page 56**, NRC family photo archives; **page 58**, NRC family photo archives; **page 61**, Paul Hartmann, Photography; **page 62**, Paul Hartmann, Photography; **page 67**, Paul Hartmann, Photography; **page 73**, Paul Hartmann, Photography; **page 75**, Photodisk; **page 77**, Photodisk; **page 78**, Photodisk; **page 81**, Photodisk; **page 84**, Paul Hartmann, Photography; **page 86**, Paul Hartmann, Photography; **page 88**, Photodisk; **page 89**, Photodisk; **page 97**, Photodisk; **page 100**, Paul Hartmann, Photography; **page 105**, Photodisk; **page 109**, Photodisk; **page 113**, Photodisk; **page 115**, NRC family photo archives; **page 116**, Photodisk; **page 121**, Photodisk; **page 122**, Paul Hartmann, Photography; **page 125**, Paul Hartmann, Photography; **page 127**, Photodisk.

The National Academy of Sciences is a private, nonprofit, self-perpetuating society of distinguished scholars engaged in scientific and engineering research, dedicated to the furtherance of science and technology and to their use for the general welfare. Upon the authority of the charter granted to it by the Congress in 1863, the Academy has a mandate that requires it to advise the federal government on scientific and technical matters. Dr. Bruce M. Alberts is president of the National Academy of Sciences.

The National Academy of Engineering was established in 1964, under the charter of the National Academy of Sciences, as a parallel organization of outstanding engineers. It is autonomous in its administration and in the selection of its members, sharing with the National Academy of Sciences the responsibility for advising the federal government. The National Academy of Engineering also sponsors engineering programs aimed at meeting national needs, encourages education and research, and recognizes the superior achievements of engineers. Dr. William A. Wulf is president of the National Academy of Engineering.

The Institute of Medicine was established in 1970 by the National Academy of Sciences to secure the services of eminent members of appropriate professions in the examination of policy matters pertaining to the health of the public. The Institute acts under the responsibility given to the National Academy of Sciences by its congressional charter to be an adviser to the federal government and, upon its own initiative, to identify issues of medical care, research, and education. Dr. Kenneth I. Shine is president of the Institute of Medicine.

The National Research Council was organized by the National Academy of Sciences in 1916 to associate the broad community of science and technology with the Academy's purposes of furthering knowledge and advising the federal government. Functioning in accordance with general policies determined by the Academy, the Council has become the principal operating agency of both the National Academy of Sciences and the National Academy of Engineering in providing services to the government, the public, and the scientific and engineering communities. The Council is administered jointly by both Academies and the Institute of Medicine. Dr. Bruce M. Alberts and Dr. William A. Wulf are chairman and vice chairman, respectively, of the National Research Council.

Index

tarting Out Right:
Guide to Promoting Children's Success in Reading

oday's children are faced with a world increasingly based on echnology. At the same time, competition in the workplace is etting tougher. If you can't read an instruction manual or nderstand a report about a trade transaction, you may be left out f the future. The good news is that most children will learn how read in almost any classroom with almost any type of reading rogram. That many children are at high risk of reading failure is e bad news—not only for them and the people who care about em but for all of American society.

tarting Out Right boils down the research findings to practical uidelines and suggestions, enhanced with many ideas and xamples. It is a "must read" for specialists in primary education s well as pediatricians, child care providers, tutors, literacy dvocates, and parents.

BN 0-309-06410-4; 192 pages, 8.25 x 10, paperbound, $14.95

Preventing Reading Difficulties in Young Children

Book Review Highlights

"Could serve as a road map to national standards."
The New York Times

"The contentious, decades-long debate about how to teach reading is over."
The Boston Globe

"The largest study of its kind ever attempted, which tackles some of the most explosive issues in education."
Newsday

ISBN 0-309-06418-X; 448 pages, 6 x 9, index, hardbound, $35.95

Use the form on the reverse of this card to order your copies today.

tarting Out Right:
Guide to Promoting Children's Success in Reading

oday's children are faced with a world increasingly based on chnology. At the same time, competition in the workplace is etting tougher. If you can't read an instruction manual or nderstand a report about a trade transaction, you may be left out f the future. The good news is that most children will learn how read in almost any classroom with almost any type of reading ogram. That many children are at high risk of reading failure is e bad news—not only for them and the people who care about em but for all of American society.

tarting Out Right boils down the research findings to practical idelines and suggestions, enhanced with many ideas and amples. It is a "must read" for specialists in primary education well as pediatricians, childcare providers, tutors, literacy vocates, and parents.

BN 0-309-06410-4; 192 pages, 8.25 x 10, paperbound, $14.95

Preventing Reading Difficulties in Young Children

Book Review Highlights

"Could serve as a road map to national standards."
The New York Times

"The contentious, decades-long debate about how to teach reading is over."
The Boston Globe

"The largest study of its kind ever attempted, which tackles some of the most explosive issues in education."
Newsday

ISBN 0-309-06418-X; 448 pages, 6 x 9, index, hardbound, $35.95

Use the form on the reverse of this card to order your copies today.

ORDER CARD
(Customers in North America Only)

Starting Out Right

Use this card to order additional copies of **Starting Out Right** and the book described on the reverse. All orders must be prepaid. Please add $4.00 for shipping and handling for the first copy ordered and $0.50 for each additional copy. If you live in CA, DC, FL, MA, MD, MO, TX, or Canada, add applicable sales tax or GST. Prices apply only in the United States, Canada, and Mexico and are subject to change without notice.

___ I am enclosing a U.S. check or money order.

___ Please charge my VISA/MasterCard/American Express account.

Number: ______________________

Expiration date: ______________________

Signature: ______________________

PLEASE SEND ME: **SOR**

Qty.	Code	Title	Price
___	START	Starting Out Right	$14.95
___	PREREA	Preventing Reading Difficulties	$35.95
		Subtotal	___
		Shipping	___
		Tax	___
		Total	___

Please print.

Name ______________________

Address ______________________

City ______________ State _____ Zip Code ___________

FOUR EASY WAYS TO ORDER

- **Electronically:** Order from our secure website at: **www.nap.edu**
- **By phone:** Call toll-free 1-800-624-6242 or (202) 334-3313 or call your favorite bookstore.
- **By fax:** Copy the order card and fax to (202) 334-2451.
- **By mail:** Return this card with your payment to NATIONAL ACADEMY PRESS, 2101 Constitution Avenue, NW, Lockbox 285, Washington, DC 20055.

Quantity Discounts: 5-24 copies, 15%; 25-499 copies, 25%. To be eligible for a discount, all copies must be shipped and billed to one address.

All international customers please contact National Academy Press for export prices and ordering information.

ORDER CARD
(Customers in North America Only)

Starting Out Righ

Use this card to order additional copies of **Starting Out Right** and the book described on the reverse. All orders must be prepaid. Please add $4.00 for shipping and handling for the first copy ordered and $0.50 for each additional copy. If you live in CA, DC, FL, MA, MD, MO, TX, or Canada, add applicable sales tax or GST. Prices apply only in the United States, Canada, and Mexico and are subject to change without notice.

___ I am enclosing a U.S. check or money order.

___ Please charge my VISA/MasterCard/American Express account.

Number: ______________________

Expiration date: ______________________

Signature: ______________________

PLEASE SEND ME: **SOR**

Qty.	Code	Title	Price
___	START	Starting Out Right	$14.95
___	PREREA	Preventing Reading Difficulties	$35.95
		Subtotal	___
		Shipping	___
		Tax	___
		Total	___

Please print.

Name ______________________

Address ______________________

City ______________ State _____ Zip Code ___________

FOUR EASY WAYS TO ORDER

- **Electronically:** Order from our secure website at: **www.nap.edu**
- **By phone:** Call toll-free 1-800-624-6242 or (202) 334-3313 or call your favorite bookstore.
- **By fax:** Copy the order card and fax to (202) 334-2451.
- **By mail:** Return this card with your payment to NATIONAL ACADEMY PRESS, 2101 Constitution Avenue, NW, Lockbox 285, Washington, DC 20055.

Quantity Discounts: 5-24 copies, 15%; 25-499 copies, 25%. To be eligible for a discount, all copies must be shipped and billed to one address.

All international customers please contact National Academy Press for export prices and ordering information.